Don

W9-BTE-912

LOVE AND
BE LOVED

"Love to a child is like sunshine to a flower, like
water to a thirsty plant, like honey to a bee.
Nothing is as important to a child's feelings of
self-worth as the knowledge that he is unequivocally
loved by the people who are most important in
his life...

"Parental love must not ebb and flow like the tides
but be lasting and permanent as the ocean itself."
—from *You and Your Child's Self-Esteem*

❧

Written with compassion and caring by James M.
Harris, Ph.D., a prominent child psychologist and
former national consultant in the Head Start program, *You and Your Child's Self-Esteem* is packed
with practical suggestions, personal anecdotes,
case histories, and insights for parents of children
of *all* ages. Himself the father of eight, the author
gives invaluable guidelines for parents who want
to correct present behavior, ward off potential
problems, and help their children to be all they
can be.

YOU AND YOUR CHILD'S SELF-ESTEEM

JAMES M. HARRIS, Ph.D.

WARNER BOOKS

A Warner Communications Company

WARNER BOOKS EDITION

This Warner Books Edition is published by arrangement with
Carroll & Graf Publishers, Inc., 260 Fifth Avenue, New York, NY 10001.

Cover design by Richard Rossiter
Cover photograph by FOUR BY FIVE

Warner Books, Inc.
666 Fifth Avenue
New York, N.Y. 10103

Ⓦ A Warner Communications Company

Printed in the United States of America

First Warner Books Printing: May, 1990

10 9 8 7 6 5 4 3 2 1

To Delores

Contents

Introduction

Suppose you had it in your power to give your child one gift—one possession or quality of supreme importance to his future success and happiness. What would you choose? Riches? Would an inexhaustible supply of money answer all his dreams? Some of the richest people in the world are also some of the most unhappy people. It is a trite, yet true, statement that money cannot buy happiness.

Perhaps the most important gift you could give to your child would be fame—his name known to everyone; adulation from people wherever he went. But there are drawbacks to being well-known. People who are in the public eye often long for more privacy: signing autographs and answering endless questions can become tedious. The personal agony in the lives of people who seem to have everything is well documented. No, fame does not necessarily bring happiness, and even if it did it is usually short-lived.

Well then, how about a gift of intelligence? Surely, being smarter than other people would help your child to be successful and happy. While intelligence, used correctly, can be a real asset to an individual and to society, used incorrectly it can bring great harm. Master criminals, in contrast to small-time crooks, are often quite intelligent, but they use their intellect to harm and destroy. Also, a person who is very bright but does not know how to get along with other people can be a misfit in society. No, intelligence per se does not guarantee success or happiness.

Perhaps the gift you would like to give your child, had you the power, would be beauty, physical health and strength, a congenial personality, or any one of a number of other qualities. But the gift that in my view overshadows them all is the gift of self-esteem.

As I have worked with my own and other children over a period of many years, I have become convinced that there are few things as important to welfare and happiness as feelings of self-worth. They are central to happiness and success in all aspects of life. And fortunately, though self-esteem is not something you can directly bestow upon your child, it is more amenable to change and growth than most of the things we have mentioned. The intent of this book is to help you to give this invaluable gift of self-esteem to your children.

How This Book Can Help

Much has been written about self-esteem in recent years. Teachers, counselors and psychologists have access to much information pertaining to children's self-esteem. There are also some good books and articles written to help adults to increase their own feelings of self-worth. But, surprisingly, very little of the available literature contains specific and concrete advice to parents for enhancing self-esteem in their own children. This book was written to fill this need.

This book is an outgrowth of over twenty-five years of professional experience as a teacher, school psychologist, consultant, college professor, and father of eight children. The examples given are almost all drawn from actual incidents involving my own children, children of friends, and children with whom I have worked. Some of these examples, for one reason or another, may not fit your own experience well. This is understandable in view of the great diversity that exists in society. But the basic principles behind the examples are true and important. Look for these principles, and apply them in your own way to your own children.

One note of explanation is in order. Throughout the book I have used the traditional "he" when referring to the child—unless I am referring specifically to a girl. I have used "she" when referring to the parent—unless I am referring specifically to a father. Though parents and children come in both sexes, it is awkward to use he/she continually. I think that such usage interferes with readability. Some authors have resorted to alternating "he" and "she" with each paragraph to avoid being sexist, but I feel that this technique is also awkward. I hope that the compromise of using the masculine pronoun for the child and the feminine pronoun for the parent is acceptable to you.

Many of the ideas and suggestions you read in these pages will not be new to you, but reminders are helpful to all of us. This book discusses well over a hundred ways to help children feel good about themselves. If you are a parent you are already doing many of these things, but almost anyone can improve.

Another note of caution. Some of the suggestions I have given may not seem reasonable, or may not fit your situation. Parents differ from one another as much as children do. What works for one parent may not work for another. Also, your children have learned to know you, just as you have learned to adjust to them, and radical changes in your behavior may be confusing to them. Ease into changes gradually, and skip things that don't make sense to you. You do not have to do everything the book says to do in order to be a good parent.

At the end of this book is a check list for parents; it lists many of the suggestions that are discussed throughout the book. You may want to turn to it now to see where you stand, and then conscientiously try to apply those suggestions that seem meaningful and reasonable. At the end of the book is a bibliography of other books about children's self-esteem that you may wish to refer to.

My wife and I make no claims to being perfect parents. Through the years we have made many mistakes in our attempts to raise happy, responsible children. But we have tried to learn from these mistakes. Though the intentions of most parents are the very best, all of us are subject to normal human errors. We can't hope to always say and do the thing that is best for a child at any given moment. Isn't it a relief to know that we don't *always* have to be right to raise normal, healthy children? A child is much more like a rubber ball than a china dish; he can bounce back again and again without breaking. In this very difficult and very crucial job of parenting we will make mistakes. But we can still be effective parents. Though you will not be able to, or perhaps even wish to, apply all the suggestions given in these pages, the more of them that you are able to implement the more you will see your children's self-esteem blossom, and the more your relationship with them will be strengthened.

CHAPTER 1

The Importance of Self-Esteem

There is no value judgment more important to man—no factor more decisive in his psychological development and motivation—than the estimate he passes on himself.
—*Nathaniel Brandon*

Self-esteem is a person's overall judgment of himself—how well he likes himself. One who has high self-esteem respects himself and considers himself worthy. One with low self-esteem constantly demeans himself and considers other people to be more important than he. It would be hard to overestimate the importance of liking oneself; it is central to success and happiness. Attempts to maintain our self-esteem guide every action of our lives; nothing is more important to our survival and feelings of safety.

There are two basic ingredients that are of all-consuming importance to self-esteem. One of these is love. To feel genuinely and completely loved, without reservation, by parents and other significant people in one's life is of incalculable benefit to building self-esteem. Individuals who lack this assurance are almost certain to have problems with self-esteem. Parents who sincerely love their children, and are able to convey this love, build self-esteem in them in a very significant way.

The other basic ingredient of self-esteem is capability. Feelings of inadequacy and helplessness contribute strongly to low self-esteem. Feelings of "I can do it by myself" make self-esteem grow. It is important that everybody find things they can do well; every success enhances self-esteem. And as self-esteem and confidence grow, one is able to proceed with more assurance as each new situation arises. A person with low self-esteem is apt to distrust his own ideas and abilities and be very tentative in dealing with life situations. A person with high self-esteem views the world with optimism, confidence, and an expectation of success.

Though it may not always seem so to an observer, people always act in ways that seem to them to be most rewarding. When a person is faced with a choice of acting or thinking in one way or another, the decision is based on which choice will best maintain or increase self-esteem. If this statement is true, why then do some people behave in ways that are irrational and self-destructive? It may be that their thought processes are disturbed or that there are some hidden needs that are so powerful that they supersede logic. Sometimes these people need to be shown more effective ways of meeting these needs—ways that will work in favor of self-esteem rather than against it.

Effects of Low Self-Esteem

It would be hard to overestimate the negative impact of low self-esteem upon individuals and upon society as a whole. Authorities have estimated that half of the people who enter doctors' offices with a physical disorder, disease, or need for surgery have more of a psychological problem than a physical one. A great majority of these people suffer from low self-esteem.

Many young people drink or take drugs to bolster feelings of confidence and self-importance, even though it is illegal for them to do so. Teenage alcoholism is a major problem in our society, more than five million teenagers use marijuana, and many are turning to even more dangerous and addicting drugs. A substantial number of them become involved to compensate for low self-esteem. Low self-regard is probably a factor in most cases of adolescent depression and suicide, and homicide as well. It is also a factor in teenage sexual promiscuity, pregnancy, and early marriage. Clearly there is a need for parents to increase their effectiveness in building self-esteem in their children.

Counterfeit Self-Esteem

Most dictionaries say very little about self-esteem. *Webster's Seventh New Collegiate Dictionary* and the *Thorndike-Barnhart Comprehensive Desk Dictionary* both define it identically as 1. self-respect; 2. self-conceit. These definitions, in addition to being quite brief, seem to conflict with one another. Self-respect seems to be appropriate, but is a person with high self-esteem really conceited? Dorothy Briggs, in her excellent book *Your Child's Self-Esteem*, says that "high self-esteem is not a noisy conceit. It is a quiet sense of self-respect, a feeling of self-worth . . . Conceit is but whitewash to cover low self-esteem."

Children cover up their lack of self-esteem in many ways. Consider these examples: Jackie constantly admires herself in the mirror. Tom loves to "lord it over" the other kids and bully those younger or weaker than he. Eric constantly puts others down and seems to think that his opinion is the only correct one. Do these children have too much self-esteem? More likely they lack positive feelings about themselves. Jackie's vanity results from basic insecurity; she would not have to look for constant reassurance in the mirror if she truly saw herself as a person of value. Tom's bullying behavior comes about because of insecurity and hostile feelings; he compensates for feelings of worthlessness by directing his aggressiveness toward safe targets. A child with a high sense of his own value has no need to push others around, especially those too little or too weak to fight back. Eric is not nearly as sure of his opinions as he would like people to believe. He covers up low self-esteem with bluster.

A person who has high self-regard does not have to push others down to make himself feel important; he does not have to monopolize every conversation. He does not always have to be "right." Respect for self and respect for others go hand in hand.

Actually, there is a relationship between self-esteem and self-love, or conceit, but the relationship is a negative one rather than a positive one. When self-esteem is threatened a person retreats into himself to bolster it up. It's as though he says to himself, "If no one else will love me I must love myself all the more."

Nathaniel Brandon, in his book *The Psychology of Self-Esteem*, states that self-esteem pertains to one's conviction of his fundamental worth, while pride pertains to the pleasure one takes in himself because of specific achievements or actions. Self-esteem is confidence in one's general ability to achieve values, while pride is the result of having achieved some particular value. Self-esteem is, "I can." Pride is, "I have."

Brandon further suggests that self-esteem is such a fundamental human need that when one fails to achieve it he may fake it and protect his ego behind a barricade of pseudo-self-esteem. This pseudo-self-esteem is maintained in two ways: by evading and denying ideas and feelings that could affect his self-appraisal negatively; and by interpreting situations and events irrationally.

Winners and Losers

For several years I coached a Little League baseball team. It was interesting to see the differences in size and coordination in the group of nine- and ten-year-old boys. Even more intriguing was the range of self-confidence. Some boys appeared to have unlimited assurance as shown in their oft-repeated cries, "Coach, let me pitch!" These were the boys who came up to bat each time fully expecting to get a hit. Other boys on the team seemed content to sit on the bench and watch the others play. When they came to bat they just knew they were going to strike out—and they did! It was as though some boys were programmed to succeed and others programmed to fail.

It was noted that the boys who were "winners" were not necessarily those with the greatest amount of size, speed, and coordination; neither were the "losers" necessarily lacking in these attributes. But the first group were the ones who made rapid improvement, and as the season wore on the gap steadily increased.

What makes some children excited, eager to try new things, and confident of success? Why are others afraid to try for fear of failure? The answer is not simple; many factors are involved. We are quite sure that the self-concept is acquired, not inherited or inborn. It develops primarily out of the relationships that a child has with immediate family and other significant persons in his life. A child feels loved, wanted, and capable to the degree that these "significant others" tell him that he is—not only in their speech, but also in the way they deal with him.

Though parents cannot assume all the credit for a child's high self-esteem, nor accept all the blame for low self-esteem, child-rearing practices do exert an important impact. We can learn to change our responses to children in ways that will enhance self-esteem.

The Child's Potential for Developing Self-Esteem

It seems apparent that some children have an easier time than others in acquiring feelings of self-worth. It was once thought by psychologists that a child came into the world like a blank tablet or a lump of clay, and that what was written on the tablet, or the shape that the clay took, was almost totally a result of environmental influence. More and more we are realizing that children are inherently different from one another—that they bring different traits and potentialities into this life. Nurses who work in hospital nurseries can attest to the fact that from the day of birth infants differ markedly in their personalities. While one lies quietly and placidly most of the time, the infant in the next crib cries lustily and kicks the covers off as quickly as the nurse can replace them. While the first is happy and content as long as basic physical needs are met, the second demands his infant rights and refuses to be ignored. While there is no assurance that these described traits will endure, the quiet infant tends to become the quiet child; the active robust infant tends to become the more active, aggressive child. While either type of child can gain self-esteem, parental approaches to bring this about will need to be different.

Some children have much more "going for them" than do others. A child who is healthy, attractive, and well-endowed physically will find it easier to develop and maintain feelings of self-worth than will a child who lacks these attributes. Nonetheless, any child can develop self-esteem with the help of parents and other significant adults.

How Self-Esteem Develops in Children

All children have a built-in need for self-esteem, but they are not born with a knowledge of what will satisfy that need; they must discover it through their experiences. These experiences begin on the day of birth. The primary care-givers, ordinarily the parents, exert the first important impact on a child's self-awareness. Later, brothers and sisters have a profound effect as well. The child's self-concept is learned and developed primarily through interaction with parents and other significant adults, siblings, and neighborhood friends. The more happy and positive these significant relationships are, the more self-worth the child will feel.

Long before an infant is able to understand words, he picks up attitudes toward himself and his world by the way he is treated. He is sensitive to the touch, facial expressions, tone of voice, and body language of those who care for him. And parents' emotional states can have a decided impact upon him. When Kirk's mother is tense or in a hurry he is fussy and uncooperative; when she's relaxed and unhurried he is peaceful and contented. Does Kirk deliberately punish the mother for not being more attentive, with an attitude, "I'll fix her!"? Of course not. He responds instinctively to her body messages.

Reflections in Parental "Mirrors"

A very significant way in which self-concept develops in children is through a process which has been called the "mirror-image concept" or the "looking-glass self." This concept says that a child comes to think of himself as he perceives that he is viewed by significant adults in his life, mainly his parents. Say, for example, that parents resent a child and view his presence as an intrusion into their lives, and they show their feelings in the way they behave toward him. Does the child correctly assess the situation and say, "If my parents were more loving people they would love me?" Probably not. More likely he says to himself, "If I were nicer (or prettier, or smarter), I would be more worthy of love; then my parents would love me." Even abused children often blame themselves for the punishment exerted by parents: "If I weren't such a bad boy/girl my dad/mom wouldn't have to get mad and hurt me."

Fortunately, as a child hears, sees, and senses that a parent views him in a positive way, he comes to see himself in that "mirror-image." It has been said that if you treat a child the way you would like him to be, there is a good chance that that is what he will become. On the other hand, if you treat a child as you are afraid he might become, you stand an equally good chance to be right.

I know a mother who continually makes comments to her daughter like these: "I'll bet you're going to leave that dirty dish in the family room!" "I'd better not catch you sneaking out without doing your homework again." "I can always count on you to stir the little kids up when I leave you in charge." As you might expect, the mother's predictions usually turn out to be correct. How much better it would be to make comments like these: "I know you'll have things in good shape when I get back. It's nice to know I don't have to be embarrassed about the house when somebody comes by unexpectedly." "I like the way you settle down and get your homework done before going out to play." "I appreciate your helpfulness with the younger children." Positive expectations and positive communication are much more effective in changing and maintaining behavior than are negative ones. And positive methods are also infinitely more effective in developing and enhancing self-esteem.

Though children have their own unique characteristics, they all have the psychological needs for feeling lovable and capable. And these needs do not end with childhood—we have them till the day we die. Meeting these needs is of vital importance at any age, and helping our children to do so is an important key to successful parenthood.

CHAPTER 2

Your Own Self-Esteem

There's only one corner of the universe you can be certain of improving, and that's your own self.

—*Aldous Huxley*

One of the most powerful influences upon our children's feelings of self-worth, perhaps the most important influence, is the example of self-esteem that parents themselves convey. It is difficult to give our children something that we do not ourselves possess.

John Martin, father of two boys, has never felt comfortable as a father, or adequate as a person. He distrusts his own judgment. He is indecisive and vacillating in his attempts at discipline, and prefers to leave such matters to his wife. Already his sons, ages seven and five, are responding to their father's lack of self-confidence by turning to their mother for direction. But their father is the main model of identification in their lives, and unless some effective intervention is made soon the boys may be on their way to becoming the same kind of personalities as their father.

A child models himself after important adults in his life and learns to think and behave as they think and behave. This process of identification is the principal way attitudes, values, and modes of behavior are learned. Though every person a child meets is a potential source of identification, parents are ordinarily those who have the greatest impact. Even though the growing child recognizes some negative qualities and traits in a parent and determines that he is not going to be that way, he frequently does adopt those same traits, seemingly without conscious effort. Alcoholics tend to come from homes where there was an alcoholic parent; child abusers almost always were subjected to abuse themselves as children.

Does what we have said mean that negative traits are inevitably and invariably passed on to children and that there is no hope of a child's becoming better than the parent? Such a view is overly pessimistic. Identification is only one way by which the child learns his role. But everything being equal, the parent who has a high degree of self-esteem is the one in the best position to help the child feel good about himself.

Improving One's Own Self-Esteem

Is it really reasonable to believe that an adult can make positive changes in feelings of self-worth? Doesn't this have to happen in childhood? Fortunately, a person can change at any age. Admittedly, the older one is, the harder it is to effect significant changes in attitude and behavior, but it can be done. Here are a few suggestions of ways to enhance your own self-esteem:

1. Concentrate on the strengths of others. The ability to

make friends and to make others like us better is contingent to a great extent on how we make them feel about themselves. People will like us if because of our association with them they feel more worthwhile, more happy or more able. They will dislike us if we make them feel inferior, stupid or unhappy. And it naturally follows that as we respond in ways that make others like us, and we perceive that they do, our feelings of self-worth are magnified.

It may appear that a person who is self-centered has too much self-esteem; but the truth is that he has too little. People who think only of themselves, and are unconcerned or unaware of the needs of others, are really struggling to see themselves as worthy individuals. Self-centeredness results from selfishness and self-pity, and leads to jealousness and a resentment of others. Those with real self-esteem give little thought to their own needs. Some real people attempt to make themselves feel important by ridiculing and demeaning others. But tearing down other people is self-defeating and nonproductive. As we respond to the good in others we free ourselves to see the good in ourselves as well.

2. Praise yourself, and focus on your good qualities. Just as it is important to see value in others, it is also important to recognize our own self-worth. Emphasize your virtues, and ignore and play down any traits or attributes that you or others may perceive as undesirable, but cannot be easily changed. A case in point is a woman whom we have known for many years who bears the name Lula Belle. Because a well-known comic strip character with this name is depicted as lacking in brightness, femininity, or other desirable characteristics, there might have been an inclination to change her name, use a nickname, or shorten it to Lu or Belle. But she uses the name proudly and with no apologies; and after knowing her a short time the name becomes not only accepted, but even tinged with the same positive feelings that the woman herself generates. Demonstrate legitimate

pride in your own accomplishments, and let your child observe the satisfaction that these accomplishments bring.

Donald Felker, in his book *Developing Positive Self-Concepts*, states that a good way for parents and teachers to enhance self-esteem in children is to teach them to praise themselves. He suggests that the best way for a child to learn to praise himself is for parents and other adults to model the behavior by praising themselves. Many adults have trouble with this concept because it seems contrary to the virtues of modesty and humility that we are taught to emulate. Certainly, some restraint and some care in the choice of settings in which to indulge in self-praise are needed. Self-praise could lead to boorishness and offensiveness if not handled correctly. Nevertheless, giving ourselves legitimate praise in the presence of children, and teaching them to do the same, is an effective way to enhance self-esteem in them and in ourselves. Statements such as "I like the way that dress turned out"; "It makes me feel good to get those shelves finished; it's really going to help our storage problem"; "I think I look good in this color"; and "I got the highest score on the midterm exam in my evening class," are good for you to make, and good for your children to hear.

Learn to accept compliments graciously. Minimize critical comments and statements about yourself as well as about others.

3. Get involved in projects and programs that lead to self-improvement and self-enhancement. The nature of the self-improvement activities that one chooses will depend on his interests and on the specific weaknesses that need strengthening. For one who is overweight it may involve the self-discipline of eating in moderation only those foods that are healthy and nutritious, and beginning an exercise program. For another person it may involve study and work to develop a talent that has lain dormant. It may mean getting

involved in a class or program designed to teach specific skills or develop certain traits, for example, assertiveness-training. As you begin a worthwhile project, and then persist and see it through to completion, your self-esteem is enhanced.

4. Assume responsibility for your own thoughts and actions. Our life is what we make it. It is our own attitudes and behaviors that bring us, or fail to bring us, success and happiness. It is very easy to blame someone else when things don't go our way. "I don't have enough self-confidence because my mother was always putting me down as a child." "I've never done very well in school because I got off to such a poor start; my first grade teacher was lousy." "My sister always bossed me around and did everything for me; I never learned to take the initiative and do things for myself." "The boss insulted me, so I quit." "I can't help being grouchy; Dad was the same way, and I inherited it from him." "I'm not the only one; everybody else does it too!" While there may be a measure of truth in statements such as these, they are self-defeating and serve as a "cop-out."

Instead of blaming other people for failure or unhappiness, one may blame situations or events. "They just filled the position. That's the way it always goes; if I'd gone in a day earlier I'd have had the job." "She *always* wins! I never saw anybody so lucky at games." "If the weather had been better we would have made it all the way." "I've been sick so much lately or I'd have gotten better grades." While we are all victims of circumstance at times, it is all too easy to make excuses for failure rather than persisting and overcoming the roadblocks that stand in our way.

Another way of escaping from responsibility is to assign ourselves a label: "I'm depressed." "I'm not very outgoing, and I have a hard time making friends." "I have a hot temper." "I'm very forgetful." "I'm not very smart when it comes to numbers."

Whenever a person avoids responsibility for his actions through blaming other people, seeing himself as the victim of circumstance, or labeling himself as being this way or that way, he fails to face squarely up to his problems. He is out of control because he feels that circumstances are controlling him rather than the other way around. The inevitable result of such attitudes is lowered self-esteem.

The first step in success is to believe that it will happen. Henry Ford said that one of the great discoveries a man makes, one of his great surprises, is to find that he can do what he was afraid he couldn't do. He suggests that the barriers to success are often within ourselves.

5. Deal wisely with the priorities in your life. Why is it that some people seem to be able to accomplish so much, while others seem to be just as busy, yet accomplish so much less? How often do you hear yourself or others say, "I just haven't had time to do it yet."? While some of us are endowed with more strength and energy, more worldly goods, and even more intelligence than others, all of us are precisely equal in one significant commodity—time. We all share equally that priceless unit of time we call a day, with its twenty-four important hours, its 1440 golden minutes that can slip away so easily and quietly, to be lost forever. So when we say, "I haven't had time," we really mean, "I haven't *taken* time."

When the storeroom in our home has been left unattended for too long, I shudder each time I open the door and say to myself, "There just isn't room for all this junk." But when my wife and I work together, in a surprisingly short time everything is organized on the shelves and there is room to spare. It's true some things are discarded in the process as we face up to the fact that the chances of actually needing some of the items we have been holding on to are really quite remote. But this accounts for very little of the extra space we find. Most of it is created by organizing the space and using it more effectively.

Organization can accomplish the same thing for time as it does for space. Unbudgeted time, like unbudgeted money, tends to slip away, and we wonder where it all went. Time spent in keeping track of how our time is spent is time well spent! A careful look may reveal some activities that are not important enough to justify the time it takes to do them. One of my wife's friends irons everything she washes—not only sheets and pillowcases, but even her dishcloths. She learned this from her mother. But she fails to consider that her mother did not have permanent press fabrics, nor a dryer that leaves clothes practically wrinkle-free. While it is very nice to sleep on freshly laundered and ironed sheets, this luxury has to be weighed against what may well be more important considerations. And the same might be said about many other household tasks.

Obviously, when we fritter away time with inconsequential things we rob from the important matters that should be occupying our thoughts and attention. Each person must define for himself what these central matters are. Unless we establish priorities and hold to them, our time is likely to be used up in nonproductive ways. I am not suggesting that one should "keep his nose to the grindstone" constantly. A half-hour spent in an enjoyable way with a child may be far more important than the same amount of time spent at the office working overtime.

Charles Schwab, a great American industrialist, was asked how he managed to accomplish so much. He described a very simple, but effective, way of budgeting his time. Each evening before retiring he would list in order of priority five things that he wanted to accomplish. The next day he would work on these five items, and usually find when the day was over that he had been able to accomplish only part of them. That evening he would again list his five most crucial objectives, repeating the unaccomplished activities if they still held priority. In this way he was always spending his time on important tasks. Others have adopted Schwab's system and found it to work for them. You may also wish to try it. Avoid procrastination. Be punctual. As you become the master of your time rather than the victim, your self-confidence will grow, and your feelings of competency and self-esteem will increase.

6. Set realistic goals. Goals that are either too low or too high mitigate against self-esteem. If a person doesn't aspire to very much, that is likely to be the level he attains, and there is little reward or feeling of accomplishment. If he aspires to too much, he is setting himself up for feelings of disappointment and failure. In either case self-esteem is likely to suffer.

Women in today's society are especially vulnerable to unrealistic goals and consequently, to lowered self-esteem. The women's movement has focused on women's rights, and rightfully so. Traditionally, women have been denied some basic rights that they should share equally with men. But as women's rights increase, expectations and responsibilities also increase—sometimes unrealistically. A generation ago the role of homemaker was considered a full-time job. If a woman kept the house in good order, prepared nutritious meals for her family, and fostered congenial relationships in the home, that is all anyone would ever expect of her. But now, in this era of labor-saving devices, where household tasks can be performed better and in much less time than formerly, and where family size is greatly reduced, it is no longer as acceptable to be "just a house-wife." There are pressures, both personal and societal, to do something more in life. But the combined responsibilities of homemaking and a career can impose an overwhelming burden. This is especially true if the husband does not see his role as having changed—if he expects his wife to hold a full-time job and yet still do everything that has been traditionally considered "women's work." In such a setting is it any wonder that the wife and mother finds that she has neither the energy nor enough hours in the day to successfully carry out the role that she and others have assigned to her? And is it any wonder that feelings of frustration and failure damage self-esteem?

In a situation such as this, both husband and wife, and children too, have to realize that when the wife works others have to share in the responsibilities that otherwise would be hers. They also have to understand that there must be some "trade-offs." In exchange for the increased income the family enjoys, home-cooked meals frequently have to give way to fast-food takeout, home-mended clothes to a trip to the tailor, or discarding them altogether; hand-ironed shirts to permanent press shirts worn directly from the dryer. And the husband may find that in an effort to ease his wife's burden he may have to take some shortcuts too. The leisurely Saturday afternoon washing and waxing of the family automobile may have to give way to taking it through a car wash as he helps with some household chore or project. The flower-bed that requires hours of tender loving care in order to bloom impressively, free of weeds, may have to be filled in with grass or with a type of foliage that fills in quickly and requires little weeding. In as complex and pressure-filled society as the one in which we live, no one can do everything he would like to do or be "all things to all people." We must either face this fact or suffer feelings of inadequacy. Avoid extremely high demands upon yourself, and do not judge yourself against a standard of unattainable objectives.

7. Value your own opinion. I have a good friend who seldom expresses a strong opinion about anything. It's interesting to engage him in conversation, or observe as he converses with others, and see how readily he can shift from

one point of view to an opposite one so as not to take a chance of causing offense. Needless to say, this man is a "sucker" for any salesman or con artist that comes along.

Do you ever set your own views aside because others appear to be more knowledgeable or more forceful? Realize that you are just as much of an authority on most issues as the people around you. While it is important to avoid "bullheadedness," do not be too quick to back down or change your opinion just because someone else sees something in a different way. As you hold to a reasonable opinion and avoid being "wishy-washy," others will respect you more and you will respect yourself as well.

8. Respect your personal rights. Do not take advantage of others, but, at the same time, do not allow others to take advantage of you. Refuse to be anyone's doormat. When a person in your home or in your automobile says "Do you mind if I smoke?," if you *do* mind, say so. When you have been waiting for a half-hour in a line and the person in front of you says, "Is it OK if my friend cuts in?," and you think it is not fair to you or others behind you, then say so. However, when you see that the person behind you in the line at the supermarket has only one or two items, and you let them go ahead of you, let it be because *you* want to be helpful. As you stand up for yourself and refuse to let others take unfair advantage, you will increase your self-respect.

9. Behave consistently with your personal standards and values. If you do not drink and do not approve of the use of alcohol, do not accept a drink merely to avoid offending others. Afterwards you may feel resentful of the pressures put upon you to drink, and guilty for responding to those pressures.

Do not let your desire for popularity, or your need to avoid embarrassment, influence your decision as to how to act. Do not compromise a principle to avoid offending someone, even though it be a good friend. Most people respect someone for holding to their standards of behavior, even those they do not personally share. Avoid hypocrisy! Violating one's own code of ethics breeds guilt feelings, which lower self-esteem.

10. Maintain good health and personal appearance. Have you ever dashed out to a store with your hair in curlers or in your work clothes, hoping that you will not meet anyone you know? Or has a neighbor ever dropped in unexpectedly when your home needs cleaning? Contrast those experiences with the feelings you have when you are well-dressed and walk into a room of people, or when someone visits unexpectedly and finds your home in perfect order.

Few of us have the personal appearance we would wish to have. We may wish that we were thinner, or taller, or had more ideal facial features or any number of other attributes. While these are things we cannot easily change, we can adjust in ways that will accentuate our best features. We can care for our hair and choose a style that complements the shape of our face. If we are a little heavy we can choose clothes that have a slimming effect. We can choose colors that contribute to our best appearance. We can learn and maintain good posture. We can smile and say hello, rather than walking around with a scowl. In these and other ways we can relate more effectively with others and feel better about ourselves.

In the same way we can maximize our physical attributes we can also take actions that will maintain good health. We can eat wisely and exercise in ways that are appropriate. We can have regular physical and dental checkups. When we feel good, and look good to ourselves and to others, our self-esteem has a good chance to blossom.

Your Spouse's Self-Esteem

Ross Williams loves his wife Dolly and is affectionate when they are alone. But when they are with other people he often teases her unmercifully and makes her the butt of his jokes. She just smiles and puts on a brave front, but feels hurt and degraded. When, later, she tries to explain how his behavior has offended and embarrassed her, Ross tells her that she needs to learn to be a better sport and not so "thin-skinned." He says their friends know he is only kidding. Though Ross fails to acknowledge any problem in his behavior, Dolly's self-esteem is diminished, and she is beginning to dread social engagements.

Children should never see parents making cruel remarks or demeaning comments about each other. In a good marriage husband and wife support each other, speak well of each other, and defend each other against the world.

Husbands and wives should build each other up; the model of behavior that they set by so doing will strengthen their self-esteem and that of their children. When parents have self-esteem, competitiveness and disharmony between them decreases, strengthening the marriage relationship and the self-esteem of all family members.

CHAPTER 3

Teach Your Child to Love and to Feel Loved

The greatest happiness of life is the conviction that we are loved—loved for ourselves, or rather, loved in spite of ourselves.

—*Victor Hugo*

Nothing is as important to a child's feelings of self-worth as the knowledge that he is unequivocably loved by the people who are important in his life. Many mistakes that we might make as parents can be overcome if our children have this knowledge. Love to a child is like sunshine to a flower, like water to a thirsty plant, like honey to a bee. Your children need to know beyond any doubt that they are lovable, and that you love them.

Maslow's Hierarchy of Human Needs

Abraham Maslow, a prominent personality theorist, suggests that basic needs are interrelated and exist in a hierarchy. The first level is the physiological needs—those that are necessary to the sustaining of life, such as food, water, and shelter. According to Maslow's theory, only when this lowest level of needs is reasonably well satisfied can an individual move on to the next level—safety or security. It's hard to feel very safe or secure when your stomach is empty. When a person feels reasonably secure he can move to the third level, which is love. The fourth level is self-esteem. Only when a person can give and receive love does he have the readiness and capacity for self-esteem.

How Love Develops in Children

A child's first experiences with love come about through interaction with the primary care-giver, which in most families is the mother. She is most often the one who feeds him when he is hungry, changes his diaper when he is wet, and picks him up when he feels a need for attention.

Imagine what it is like to be totally helpless. What would it be like to be unable to talk, or to move from place to place? Some have speculated that at birth, when the infant leaves the protected and constant environment of the womb, the world must be a "buzzing mass of confusion." He cannot at first find any meaning in the stimuli which bombard him through his five senses.

But very early in life the infant begins to separate himself from his environment. He begins to be aware that the appearance of the same friendly faces occur simultaneously with physical gratification or the removal of pain and discomfort. Of course this love and comfort continues on through early childhood, and to some degree through life. Is it any wonder that parents come to be seen as the major source of love and care?

A sense of psychological well-being is enhanced as parents kiss and cuddle the child, and talk and sing to him. Bonding occurs, and feelings of love are generated.

Years ago a study compared infants born to women in prison, who were allowed to keep their babies with them, to infants raised in an orphanage. Hygiene factors in the prison were far from ideal, while the orphanage presented an antiseptic environment for the control of infectious diseases. The prison mothers were allowed to personally care for their infants and hold and cuddle them as often as they liked. In the orphanage trained nurses administered to the physical needs of the infants, but there was little holding or cuddling or other social attention. In which of these two environments were the babies more healthy? Interestingly, the prison babies were generally healthy, while the orphanage babies were often listless and sickly. It is evident that physical closeness is vital to the physical and psychological welfare of children from a very early age.

The Effects of Love Deprivation

The unfortunate infant who is denied close physical interaction with a primary care-giver is apt to develop what has been called "marasmus," or "failure to thrive." This condition is especially likely if the infant has had close physical contact that is removed without a parent substitute being provided. Even though food and physical care are readily available, the infant wastes away and may actually die. Psychological nurturing and physical cuddling are almost as essential to survival as is food!

As the child grows older, physical contact becomes less important, and, in fact, too much of it may be harmful. Physical contact is gradually replaced with emotional stimulation and social interaction. Appropriate hugging and kissing, of course, are still important at any age. As children are treated with kindness and attention, feelings of lovability increase and feelings of self-worth are enhanced.

Children who are denied love in their early years of life may develop a condition called "affect hunger"—an insatiable need for love. Even as adults they may not be able to accept the fact that they are loved. The feeling of being unlovable can lead to promiscuity, the need for a new relationship, a new conquest, in order to prove to themselves that they are worthy of love. And yet they never really believe it; their irresponsible behavior further decreases feelings of self-worth.

A girl with low self-esteem may believe that the only way she can be liked by boys is by granting sexual favors. A boy with low self-esteem may try to bolster his confidence and feelings of self-worth by seducing one girl after another. Behind his facade, the typical Don Juan is not the self-assured and irresistible person he tries to portray. Sexual promiscuity in either partner is not likely to build feelings of self-esteem. More likely it will lead to feelings of guilt which decrease self-esteem even more.

Another way that a child reacts to a feeling of not being loved is to resist adult authority. The misbehaving child is often a discouraged child. Though it is much easier to love children who do the things we want them to do than to love children who rebel, it is the misbehaving child who needs our attention—the unlovable child who most needs our love.

A child who does not feel loved may respond in a variety of other ways. He may be very timid and quiet; he may lash out in anger against his family, and against the whole world; or he may pretend not to care. But whatever the outward appearance, a child who feels unloved is not likely to be able to generate healthy feelings of self-worth.

Teach Love by Example

It has been said that the greatest gift a man can give to his children is the knowledge that he loves their mother; it is equally important for them to know that the mother loves their father. It is good for a child to see parents on occasion holding hands or kissing. The knowledge that parents love each other supplies security and a feeling that he is also loved. It also provides a model for the child to use later in communicating feelings of love to others.

Do Not Control Children by Withholding Love

Mrs. Hansen has found that a very effective way to make her daughter Margo do what she is told is to withdraw her love and support when she misbehaves. When Margo was little and did something to get recognition, her mother's common response was, "Mommie doesn't like little girls who show off." When she did something "wrong" she would hear, "Mommie doesn't love you when you are bad." So at a very early age she learned to stay in the background and do those things that would result in maternal approval. Now that she is older, Margo is still "Mommie's good girl." She does what she is told because mother's approval, and love, is so important to her. But she doesn't have much sense of her own value.

Parents are sometimes tempted to control children's behavior by withholding love because on the surface it may appear to be effective, as in the case of Margo. Children may be willing to do almost anything to keep parental love from being withdrawn. But though behavior may improve, at least temporarily, feelings of confidence and lovability erode and self-esteem diminishes. Children need to know that parents love them even when their behavior is unacceptable. We should try to separate our children from their actions, and let them know it is their behavior we dislike, not them. Parental love must not ebb and flow like the tides, but be lasting and permanent as the ocean itself.

Don't Be Afraid to Express Your Love

A middle-aged woman talked to me about her relationship with her mother, a seventy-five-year-old woman who has been a widow for almost forty years. Her mother lives 200 miles away, and this woman calls her at least once a week and goes to help her with the house and yard work once a month. She said, "You know, I love my mother of course, but it's very hard for me to say it to her. I just can't get the words out. I think the reason it's so hard to say 'I love you' is that I so seldom heard those words when I was growing up. My mother almost never told me she loved me, and now those words just don't come naturally."

The woman further confided that she finds it difficult to say, "I love you" to her husband, though she does love him deeply. The same problem carries over to her three children. Recently she has become aware of how seldom she puts her arm around them or tells them she loves them, and she is trying hard to improve. She said, "As a child I sometimes wondered if my mother really loved me. I don't want my children to have to wonder about my love for them."

Why do some people find it so hard to express their love for their children? Sometimes it is out of embarrassment, or concern for how the child will react. The kind of home that a person comes from, and the amount of love, affection, and warmth that prevailed there, has much to do with one's ability to express love.

Mrs. George was raised in a home where outward displays of affection were rare among family members, even between parents and children. Her husband, on the other hand, came from a home where brothers and sisters and parents freely embraced and kissed each other. One of the greatest adjustments the Georges have faced in their marriage is this difference in outward emotional expression. Mrs. George feels uncomfortable around her husband's family with all the "gushy" feelings that are expressed, and she doesn't want to be kissed by anyone but her husband. Conversely, Mr. George thinks that his wife's family members are a "bunch of cold fish." Unfortunately, this difference in childhood rearing has created some difficulties in relating to their children. The husband's very free emotional expression has made the wife's "coldness" all the more apparent. It is safe to say that Mrs. George loves her children just as much as her husband does, but she has difficulty in showing it.

If you were raised in a home similar to that of Mr. George, hugging and kissing your children will probably come naturally. But if your home was more like that of Mrs. George, you may need some help in learning to be more free with outward emotional expression. Appropriate physical displays of affection can enhance children's self-esteem, but the acts must be sincere and heart-felt. Children are adept at recognizing phony responses, and they feel manipulated and "turned-off" by them; the effect is to lower self-esteem rather than raise it. Parents need to work to overcome whatever barriers stand in the way of communicating to their child a deep and abiding love. A child who feels unloved is a lonely and miserable child indeed.

Don't Be Afraid to Say It!

Golde, in *Fiddler on the Roof*, is asked by her husband, "Do you love me?" She replies, "What a foolish question!

For 25 years I've washed your clothes, cooked your food, and borne your children." Her husband persists and says, "That isn't what I asked. I just want to know, Do you love me?" Finally, after another attempt or two on his part, her resistance breaks down, and she says, "I suppose I do."

Parents also may assume that acts of kindness, support, and duty are enough to show love for their children. But our children need to hear us say we love them, and to hear it often. They also need to know that we are absolutely sincere when we say it. Think for a moment! How long has it been since you told your children that you love them? Don't let another day go by—tell them today. If you feel embarrassed, or are afraid of embarrassing them, practice saying it to yourself a few times; then gather up your courage and try it out at an appropriate moment.

If you haven't made a practice of saying, "I love you" to your children, you may confuse them at first—especially teenagers. They may think you are sarcastic, or are trying to manipulate them. But as you persist and they see you are sincere and have no ulterior motive, you may be astonished at the improved attitudes of family members. In such a setting self-esteem is certain to be enhanced.

Love Children for Themselves, Not for Their Accomplishments

The two main ingredients of self-esteem are feelings of being loved and feelings of being capable. But these two sets of feelings should be maintained separately; one should not hinge on the other. It would be unfortunate and sad for a child to feel lovable only if capable. Children need to feel cherished just for being themselves, apart from their accomplishments.

Mr. Bradley teaches physical education and does some coaching at a high school. He was quite an athlete when in high school, and he has hoped that all of his children would enjoy sports competition. One of his sons, Kyle, has a muscular build and loves to compete in all kinds of sports. Paul, the other son, looks more like his mother, who is small and delicate. He lacks either the talent or the inclination to go out for any sport; further, his brother's far greater aptitude for sports discourages Paul and contributes all the more to his lack of interest. Because of Kyle's and Mr. Bradley's common interest in athletics they are thrown together in close contact regularly and frequently, while Paul has little to do with his father. If you were to ask Mr. Bradley which of his sons he loves most, he would of course say that he loves them equally—and perhaps he does. But somehow the pride and attention that he gives to Kyle's athletic prowess is a sign to Paul that since he is not as capable, he is also less important to his father and not loved to the same degree as Paul.

Paul has his own talents, and it would be well for his father to attend his jazz band concerts and school plays, even though they do not have as much personal appeal as Kyle's football games. But above all, Mr. Bradley should make it very clear that neither son's capability has anything whatever to do with their being loved just for themselves.

Our Charge as Parents

How quickly the years go by! How short the time that parents have to be the major influence in their children's lives. All too soon they will be leaving and establishing homes of their own. We may not realize how fully we love our children until the house is empty and quiet. We need to make good use of the time we have. As we strengthen the bonds of love among family members, self-esteem will flourish in our homes.

CHAPTER 4

Boost Your Child's Feelings of Importance

The deepest urge in human nature is the desire to be important.

—John Dewey

Dale Carnegie, in his well-known book *How to Win Friends and Influence People*, says that of all the human needs, the one that is seldom gratified is what Sigmund Freud calls "the desire to be great." Yet this longing is almost as important as the desire for food and sleep. Carnegie suggests that we visualize each person we meet as though carrying a sign on his chest saying, "I want to feel important."

What better friends to win and influence than our own children; yet, unless we are very careful, we may sometimes undermine rather than encourage feelings of importance. Here are some examples: A college woman refused to wear shorts because she had the "world's ugliest legs." She knew because her mother had told her so. A father undermined his son's feelings of importance by ridiculing any new or creative ideas. A father persuaded his daughter not to run for a school office because she had "no chance" against the better qualified candidates.

Examples of parents' undermining feelings of importance abound. But, fortunately, it is also easy to find situations in which children's feelings of importance are fostered and maintained despite weakness or infirmity: the very plain girl with a smile that "lights up the world," and a personality to match; the boy who is the smallest in his class but confidently participates in sports and other activities; the girl whose aptitude for school work is somewhat limited, but still tries hard and turns in all assignments. Behind such children there is likely to be a warm and loving home, with parents who react with neither scorn nor pity, but accept their children as persons of value and capability.

The Danger of Invidious Comparisons

Clark, a college freshman, told his counselor that he was looking for a field that didn't require much of an intellectual challenge because he just wasn't good at school work; yet an intelligence test revealed an IQ well above average. Clark had been continually contrasted with his two brilliant older brothers who had graduated from a prestigious university with honors. The parents treated Clark almost as though he were retarded; it was not difficult to see why he had such a low opinion of himself.

Parents too often make comparisons among their children, sometimes openly and directly: "Why can't you be as responsible as Paul?" "You'd be prettier if you fixed your hair like Kristi." But often it is made in such a subtle way that the parent doesn't even realize that such a comparison has been made. Often the intent is to set up a good example: "If you practice every day, you may get to be as good on the violin as Mike." "Study hard and you can get on the honor roll like Teresa." But it's not fair to expect a child who has his own set of talents to compete with a sibling who may have quite different attributes, especially if the other child is older. The message may come through to the child all too clearly, "I am not nearly as lovable and capable, nor as important, as my brother or sister."

When parents make invidious comparisons it is usually to encourage a younger child to look up to an older one, but sometimes it is the younger one that is presented as the model. It is hard enough for a child to try to live up to the example of an older brother or sister. But what is especially galling is to have a younger sibling put up on a pedestal.

Sometimes it is the child who compares himself in a negative way with a brother or sister. He needs to have reassurance that he enjoys the same love from parents that the competing child does, and that he is loved for himself, not for what he can or cannot do. At the same time he needs to have his own unique interests and talents developed and called to his attention. Parents would do well to comment frequently that everyone has his own abilities and should develop them rather than always doing the same things brothers and sisters do.

Highlight Your Child's Accomplishments

An acquaintance recalled a time as a young boy of six or seven when an electrician came to the house to do some rewiring. He needed to string some wire in a little crawl space too small to accommodate an adult, and he asked the boy to go in and pull the wires through. When the job was finished he handed the boy a quarter, and the proud boy went to show it to his mother. Her response was, "Oh, a quarter is too much! Go back and tell him a dime is plenty!'' This experience was repeated when he was paid for helping a neighbor bring a cow down from the pasture, and the mother sent him to return part of the money. No doubt the mother was only trying to be fair to the electrician and to the neighbor, but the fact that the incidents were recalled so clearly after a quarter of a century is telling. The effect of these and similar incidents was to lower self-esteem. How much better it would have been for the mother to say, ''Oh, a quarter is a lot of money. You must have done a good job!'' After all, the boy's feelings about himself were much more important than the possible wrong of accepting too much money.

Whenever you recognize your children's accomplishments and make them feel good that you noticed, you enhance self-esteem. But the praise must be sincere; children are quick to detect insincere flattery.

Emphasize the Good

Dale Carnegie relates an experience that a man in one of his classes told. A group of women in his church, including his wife, were involved in a self-improvement program. She asked him to help her by listing six things she could do to be a better wife. He said, ''Let me think about it and give you an answer in the morning.'' The next morning he got up early and called the florist and had six red roses sent to his wife with this message: ''I can't think of six things I would like to change about you. I like you just the way you are.'' That night he returned home to find his wife waiting at the door with tears in her eyes. And the next Sunday at church several women came up to him and said, ''That was the most considerate thing I have ever heard.''

A positive approach can be equally successful with children. When a child completes a job the human tendency is to point out the weak areas so they will improve next time. But this may discourage the child and make him less willing to try again. It is much better to comment on the parts of the performance that were done well. Suppose your daughter vacuums several rooms in the house, and all but one are done well; she "runs out of steam," and takes some shortcuts in the last room. What will happen if you ignore entirely the rooms that are done well and concentrate on the one that was done poorly, with a comment such as, "I should have known I couldn't rely on you to finish a job! Look at that lint in the corner; and how about that bobby pin you didn't even bother to pick up!" Would such comments stimulate your daughter to try harder next time? More likely they would lead to discouragement and a reluctance to try again. But if you focus on a job done well, you protect your daughter's feelings of importance.

Let's put ourselves into a similar situation. Suppose we have just spent the entire day cleaning the house from top to bottom except for one room we didn't have time to get to. Or suppose we have weeded the entire garden except for one small section. How would it make us feel if our spouse should say, "Boy, the utility room sure is a mess! How can you stand to work in all that clutter?" or "I was just out in the carrot patch, and I couldn't find the carrots for all the weeds." Would such statements make us want to rush right back and complete the work? Or would they cause feelings of resentment and hostility?

If we are never quite satisfied with the way our children perform expected tasks and continually point out how they should have been done, we discourage them and make them think they can't do anything right. We need to realize that our children will generally not perform at an adult level, nor is it logical to expect them to do so. When they do their best we need to reward them with sincere praise, and by all means we should resist the temptation to show them how much better we can do it. As we help our children to feel capable their feelings of importance and self-esteem will be enhanced.

It is important that children see the things they do around the house as making a contribution to the family—not just busy work. Even difficult and onerous tasks will be accepted cheerfully by a child who feels a sense of importance in the parental request—who feels that the parent chose him because he would do a satisfactory job.

Create Opportunities for Your Child to Win

Winning at contests and games can boost a child's feelings of importance. A mother asked me if she and her husband should deliberately lose at games so their children could experience feelings of success and the thrill of winning. It's not a bad idea for a parent to put forth less effort sometimes so the child can win. It's no fun to lose all the time, and winning can be good for a child's ego. But the older the child the more difficult it is to let them win without their being aware of the subterfuge. Turn to games where chance rather than skill and experience is the main dimension. Then your child will automatically win a share of the time.

I used to go to the gym frequently with my son, when he was about fourteen, to practice shooting the basketball and play some "one-on-one." For his age he was an excellent shooter. But because of my experience and size I could probably have won every time, blocking most of his shots. What I did was guard him loosely so he could get off his shots. I never deliberately missed the basket, but took my shots a little beyond my range when I got ahead, and close shots and lay-ins when my son was ahead. This kept the game interesting and close, and the winner was often the one who happened to hit the last basket.

You may want to try this idea of giving your child a handicap in games you play together—batting or playing Ping-Pong left-handed, for example. You will probably find, as I did, that all too soon you won't have to give a handicap; in fact, you may have to exert an all-out effort to win your share of the time.

It's fun to win, but your children need to understand that no one wins all the time. They need to learn to lose gracefully. They also need to see you win. Let's face it! If Mom and Dad always lose they may begin to appear inept; and an inept parent is not the image we hope to create for our children.

Support Your Children's Activities

Brent and Brad are neighbors and good friends. They participate in many out-of-school activities together, including scouting and sports. Brent's parents are always present when he is in a game, a school program, or receiving an advancement in scouting. Whatever the activity they are there to cheer him on. Brad's parents, on the other hand, are often too busy to attend his activities, and they don't think their presence is really all that vital. By failing to provide support they miss many opportunities to make Brad feel important and to enhance his self-esteem.

When your children participate in any activity to which parents are invited, make the effort to be there. Whether it is a leading role in the play or a bit part; whether she is a main-stringer on the team or a third-stringer; whether he is a soloist or only a member of the chorus—let them know their activities are important to you and you will add to their feelings of importance and self-esteem.

Respect Your Child's Opinions

It's easy to think when our children are young and immature that their ideas are less important than adult ideas. But this is not really so. We need to listen respectfully to our children; when we do we will often be astonished at the insight and creativity that they display. Few things will have as much value to a child's feeling of importance as the knowledge that parents think he is bright and capable.

Karl was concerned about an issue in his community. He discussed it with his parents, and with their encouragement wrote a letter to the editor of the local paper. His social studies teacher saw the letter and complimented him in class, and this touched off a lively discussion. Under the teacher's direction the class made up a questionnaire and administered it to a number of families in the community. A newspaper reporter became interested and wrote an article for the paper, and later the town council took action to remedy the situation. What a boost it was to Karl's feeling of importance!

Think what it might have been like if Karl's parents had not encouraged him to write the letter to the editor, but instead had ridiculed his views. A rich opportunity to build feelings of importance and enhance self-esteem would have been lost.

Include Your Children in Family Decisions

David, though only six and the youngest member of his family, holds his own very well with his brothers and sisters. His parents have tried hard to see that neither they nor his siblings baby him or make him feel less important than other family members. His first reaction when faced with a challenging task is to proceed on his own with confidence, but he feels comfortable in asking for help from parents or siblings if he needs it. When the time comes for family decisions that involve the children, whether it be the kind of wallpaper to put in the kitchen or where to go on a family vacation, David's opinion is considered along with the rest.

Some families hold family meetings on a regular basis, weekly or monthly. This is a good way to share ideas, bring problems out into the open and discuss issues that affect family members. Involving children in family decision making is a good way to foster feelings of importance. We are not suggesting that children be allowed to overrule or outvote parents. That would be pushing the idea of a democratic home too far. Also, many family matters are not subject to negotiation, and decisions need to be made directly by parents themselves. But when it is appropriate for children to be involved, they should feel that their suggestions have been taken seriously and fully considered before the final decision is made.

You may find that a weekly or monthly family meeting is not practical in your home. It is more likely to work when your children are young, since teenagers have a need to be away from home a lot, doing things with friends. With family members often scattering in many directions, it may be a challenge just to get everyone together for the evening meal, let alone an extra meeting. If so, try to make the meal itself a time for family discussion and decision making. If you are able to manage family meetings, you will probably find that they provide an extra opportunity for the development of feelings of closeness and family solidarity.

Make Special Days Really Special

My wife loves birthdays, holidays and special occasions.
It is traditional that when any of our children has a birthday
they get to select the family breakfast. They wake up in the
morning to the sight of balloons hanging from the chande-
lier and signs saying HAPPY BIRTHDAY. After school their
friends are invited to a birthday party. In the evening, in
addition to the usual birthday cake and opening of gifts, the
"birthday boy/girl" is consulted about the form of entertainment that they want the family to participate in. And Dad
takes movies of the major events of the day. It is rewarding
in future years for the family to spend an evening viewing
the movies, and the children will make requests such as,
"Show the one of me on my eighth birthday." Caring
enough to take pictures on birthdays and other occasions
adds to our children's feelings of importance.

There are many events in our children's lives that allow
us to pay them special attention, such as school graduations,
church ceremonies, honor awards, music recitals, athletic
contests, and others. Treating each of these events as important, and setting aside other things in order to be able to
celebrate them, tells a child that he is important to us.

Express Appreciation

Paul Harvey, in one of his "The Rest of the Story" radio
broadcasts, told about a teacher in Detroit who asked a boy
in her class, Stevie Morris, to help her find a mouse that
was lost in the classroom. The interesting part of the story is
that Stevie was blind. The teacher realized that nature had
given Stevie a remarkable set of ears to compensate for his
lack of sight. This was the first time that Stevie could

remember anyone having shown appreciation for this wonderful sense of hearing, and years later he said that this act of appreciation was the beginning of a new life. From that time on he developed this gift of hearing and went on, under the stage name of Stevie Wonder, to be a great pop singer and songwriter.

We need to remember to express appreciation to our children, and give sincere praise for their accomplishments. Too often we criticize when they do something wrong and say nothing when they do something right; and we need to do just the opposite. I am not suggesting that we flatter our children insincerely; that is counterproductive. But if we pay attention we will find abundant things about our children that we can sincerely praise.

CHAPTER 5

Encourage Independence in Your Child

You cannot teach a man anything; you can only help him to find it within himself.

—*Galileo*

There is a story told of a young man applying for a job on a farm. The farmer asked what special talent or ability the young man had. He answered, "I can sleep when the wind blows." That answer puzzled the farmer; but, feeling there was something special about the boy, he hired him. He found him to be a very capable and reliable worker. One night there was a tremendous thunderstorm with a high wind and torrential rain. The farmer ran into the room where the hired hand slept to wake him, but all of his shouting and shaking failed to arouse him. In a huff he threw on his hat and raincoat and ran out to take care of the animals himself. To his pleasant surprise he found the haystacks securely covered and tied down, the animals all inside with sufficient food and water, and everything else securely in place. A feeling of contentment came over him as the words of the young man came into his mind: "I can sleep when the wind blows."

How comforting it is for a parent to be able to "sleep when the wind blows." When your son or daughter leaves home for college, the armed forces, employment, or marriage, it will give you a feeling of security to know that your child has the fortitude and confidence to face the challenges that lie ahead. Facing what life has to offer can be an exciting opportunity rather than a dreadful experience for a child. The best way to ensure that it will be is to teach him in a way that will help develop confidence, independence, and feelings of self-respect from his earliest years.

The Importance of Early Stimulation and Experience

Feelings of independence and confidence can begin to develop in a child from a very early age. The process of setting a child free should be a gradual one, and it should begin early in life.

Mrs. Willard was puzzled when in the course of getting her fourteen-month-old daughter Wendy ready for bed the child began to kick and scream and appear to be very angry, for no apparent reason. Finally she was able to figure out that she had pulled off Wendy's socks rather than let the toddler, who had just recently learned to pull off her socks, do it for herself. Only when she put the socks back on so Wendy could pull them off again was the child comforted and placated. Isn't it interesting how early in life the need to be capable and independent emerges?

Each time a young child learns to do something new, he wants to repeat it over and over and over. Have you ever watched a toddler who has learned to go up the stairs, but not down? How many times a day does he scramble up the stairs, and then sit and cry or call for the mother to come and help him down the stairs? A busy mother may resent the child's intrusions, but the practice he gets by repeating is very important to the child's mastery of the task and to his feelings of self-esteem. It can be rewarding and exciting for a parent to watch each new accomplishment and to see the pleasure and self-confidence that it generates.

Critical Periods of Development

Child development specialists have found that there are prime periods for each type of development—a time when readiness is at a high point. For example, the critical period for motor development is between ages one and four. A child who is not encouraged to develop his physical abilities during this time finds it much harder to become proficient later on. The critical period for intellectual development is from birth to age three. It makes sense to stimulate the mind of a child very early in life; to wait until school entrance at age five or six is to wait too long. Interactions with parents in the toddler and preschool years can be crucial to later development, and mothers and fathers should allow nothing to take priority over such contact.

The critical period for the emergence of self-esteem is from about six months to eighteen months. The main catalyst is, of course, the primary care-giver, usually the mother. Children are enthralled by her every word and action. Parents are largely responsible for the self-image that the young child develops; and this self-image has a dramatic effect on ability to interact with others throughout life. Wise parents combine verbal and intellectual stimulation with social stimulation, even during the infancy stage, by talking and singing to children while cuddling them on their laps; by showing them simple books and objects of all kinds, and in numerous other ways. Such stimulation enhances not only verbal and intellectual abilities, but self-esteem as well. By age three a child is already on the way to becoming the kind of person he will be for life.

But what if your children are beyond the age of three and you have not provided the early stimulation and encouragement that promote independence and self-esteem? Is it too late? *It is never too late.* You will just have to work at it a bit harder. Even an adult can be helped to develop more initiative and self-confidence to the enhancement of self-esteem.

Develop Realistic Expectations for Your Children

A father came to talk to me about concerns that he had for his six-year-old son who was "lazy" and wouldn't do his work. It became evident that the father was expecting too much from a boy of this age, but when I tactfully suggested this idea to him he said, "I don't think I'm expecting too much. All I ask him to do is feed the dog, take care of the garbage, make his bed, keep his room picked up, and not have to be reminded every day." While to the father the tasks were very simple, to the young boy they were overwhelming, especially since he was expected to perform without any reminders or help from parents.

Just as we sometimes expect too much from our children, sometimes we expect too little. Either overly high or overly low expectations can discourage a child. As this occurs the child becomes less self-confident and less willing to do things on his own. If we force learning too early, children are not motivated and do not learn well, and feelings of confidence and capability decrease. But if we delay the opportunity for learning a skill for too long, our children learn to be dependent upon us and fail to develop the initiative and capability that is essential to feelings of self-worth.

But how can we know whether our expectations for a child are realistic? One way is to compare them with children of the same age, either directly or by consulting developmental norms established by child specialists. For example, we know that most children learn to walk between 11 and 15 months of age. By age three most children begin to put words together to form simple sentences. But these are only averages, and our children may be either slower or faster than the norm—either in general or in a specific area of development.

Another way to judge readiness in our children is to be aware of sequences of learning tasks. Though children differ greatly in rate of development, the sequence of development tends to be much the same from child to child. Children crawl before they learn to walk; they learn individual words before they say phrases and simple sentences; they can pull off their socks and shoes before they can put them on. So to some extent we can predict the tasks our children are ready for by what they have already accomplished.

Another good way to know when our children are ready for specific developmental tasks is to watch for signs of interest. Chris began to come around quite often and watch when his father was working in his shop. He would ask what this tool and that tool were for. Then he began to ask if he could try. The father could have easily squelched the boy and gotten him "out of his hair" by telling him he was too young and to go and play. Instead he did exactly the right thing by giving simple explanations and letting Chris try out some of the tools. Not only did Chris develop his mechanical skills earlier and at a higher level than most boys his age, but also his relationship with his dad was enhanced.

When your young child wants to take the spoon out of your hands and says "Me do!", he is ready to learn to feed himself. When he becomes interested in the toilet and in his own bowel movements he is ready for toilet training. When your child wants to dress himself let him do as much as possible, tactfully supplying help with buttons and zippers. When he wants to "help" with the dishes, don't say, "You're too little." Instead, find one of the simpler aspects of the job that the child can handle and let him do it. Then be sure to compliment him when he is finished and thank him for his help. The more successful experiences a child has when he is growing up, the more confidence he will have to strike out on his own.

Encourage Attempts at Self-Reliance

Suppose you were to come home from the grocery store to find the table set for dinner, and your six-year-old daughter standing by with a big smile on her face. You notice that the positions of the forks and the spoons are reversed, and she has used a motley assortment of glasses. Think of the possible approaches that might be used, and the effect of each upon the child's self-esteem and willingness to take such initiative again.

"Dear, you're a little too young to set the table. Here, let Mommy show you how."

"It just makes more work for me when you set the table. Now I have to change the silverware around and put the glasses back and get the right ones. Ask someone to help you next time."

"Now, you know that Mommy has told you not to get glasses out of the cupboard yourself. It's a wonder you didn't break one!"

How quickly you take away the thrill of surprising you and deflate the child's ego by any of the above statements. The best approach of course would be to show appropriate surprise, and then thank her for helping, saying nothing at all about the errors. Then, at another time, you could explain that it really looks nice when all the glasses are just alike and that usually the fork goes on the left side of the plate and the knife and spoon on the right. In our zeal to see something done correctly, we should not overlook the fact that the child did take the initiative to perform the task in the first place.

Don't Do Anything for a Child That He Can and Should Do Himself

If we want our children to be self-reliant we should refrain from taking over and doing things for them because we can do them better and faster. Sometimes a parent's decision on whether or not to allow a child to do something for himself is based on how much time it takes, or how much of a mess is likely. A mother might say to her four-year-old, "Here, let me pour the milk for you, darling! It's a bit heavy and you might spill it." The risk of the milk being spilled is small in comparison to the value of conveying to children that we see them as competent. It would clean up easily if it did spill, and it could provide a teaching opportunity as the child learns to clean it up.

A parent should be delighted to see a child performing beyond expectations. But occasionally a mother or father is threatened by the child's initiative. If a parent has a strong need to control or to nurture, the child's autonomy may not be a welcome development. In many ways, sometimes subtle, such a parent may actively discourage initiative and independent action, and lose a rich opportunity for the child's self-esteem to be enhanced.

Mrs. Andrews assigns each of her three children a job to do each day that is commensurate with his age, and four-year-old Thomas is no exception. He finds his name up on the chart with the other names, and often asks another family member to read to him what his job for the day is. When it is done he comes to Mom or Dad and asks for a sticker that he can paste below his name. His face beams with pride as he counts the number of consecutive days he has successfully completed his chores. When he runs into difficulty he is persistent because he knows that it is *his* job to do and that no one will come to bail him out. And he can expect parental praise and attention, which will further boost his self-esteem.

Be Patient and Noncritical

The father of a ten-year-old watched his son pitch a Little League game. It was not one of the boy's best days, and the father squirmed as he tried to sit on the bench and refrain from calling out directions. Then it occurred to him to compare mentally his son's performance with his own baseball skills at the same age, and he had to admit to himself that his son was probably as good, if not better. He also remembered that he had good days and bad days when he was a boy.

Negative criticism is nonproductive and ego deflating. Positive comments about what is done well are motivating; they build self-esteem and encouragement to move ahead.

Allow and Encourage Your Child to Explore His World

Children have so much to learn, and it's amazing how quickly they do learn. Parents should be happy when children are inquisitive; curiosity makes them effective learners and more interesting people. But sometimes parents are annoyed because of the trouble and inconvenience that arises from a child's natural curiosity and desire to explore.

On a beautiful summer day Mrs. Clemmons took her son Allen on a walk around the block. The three-year-old seemed delighted to be out of the house, and he took this opportunity to explore his world. He seemed to have a need to go up every neighbor's sidewalk, and his mother was impatient with the extra time that was involved. She longed for a leash she could put him on as time after time she called to him to return to the main path, and time after time she was ignored. She was perturbed when he picked up a dry leaf and put it into his mouth, and dismayed when he managed to find the one mud puddle in the neighborhood. She thought about all the things she had to do and regretted the decision to take her child on a walk. She did not see this as the rich learning situation it was for Allen. There were so many things for this toddler to be interested in and to learn from.

Contrast Mrs. Clemmons's overprotective behavior toward her child with Mrs. Allred and her son Kevin. When they go for a walk she lets the boy take the lead. She allows herself plenty of time and considers that the more sensory stimulation Kevin gets, the better. She expects him to get dirty, and knows that he will need a change of clothing when they arrive back home.

Children do not learn in a vacuum. The more "hands on" experience we can give them, the more quickly they will learn about their world, and, to a degree, how to control it. And the more appropriate freedom we allow, the more chance for them to become independent and self-reliant.

Allow a Certain Amount of Disorder

The mother who thinks that the most important thing in the world is to maintain a clean and orderly house with "a place for everything, and everything in its place," may have trouble coping with a toddler or young child. I am not suggesting that the best home is one that is disorderly—only that the natural tendency of a young child is not to value cleanliness and order, and too much stress on it may only frustrate him. It may seem to the mother that the child is doing all that he can to make her life difficult. But she should not take the behavior personally. What she may see as "messing up the house" may only be the child's attempt to explore the world and find out how things work.

Mrs. Howard had only been gone from the room for a few minutes when she heard a thumping sound. She had left Jason, her 14-month-old child, sitting on the kitchen floor, and she rushed back in to find a veritable disaster area. Jason was sitting in the middle of a pile of oatmeal and flour which he had pulled from a lower shelf. For good measure he had tipped over a can of honey, making the thumping sound, and the golden honey was running over the mixture of ingredients and over Jason himself. This was only the worst of several incidents that day, and Mrs. Howard could not contain her anger. "You naughty boy! What am I ever going to do with you?" She punctuated her scolding with a healthy slap of both of his hands, and then whisked him off to the bathroom for the third major cleanup of the day.

How could Jason have predicted that the activities that were so interesting to him would make his mother so angry? Upset and confused, he had no concept at all of the fact that it was his exploratory behavior that brought on her anger. As his mother over-controls Jason and continually discourages independent action, he may grow to be unsure of himself and inhibit independent and creative responses.

Mr. and Mrs. Dabakis know that it is not in the natural order of things for young children to always be neat and orderly. They maintain a basement area in their home where children can busy themselves to their hearts content with anything and everything, and where they do not always have to put things away that they plan to use later. The regular rooms of their home are "child-proofed"—expensive, breakable, and dangerous items are put away, out of the children's sight and reach. When three-year-old Marcus opens up a lower kitchen cupboard, drags out the pots and pans, and clatters them about, Mother is unperturbed, and waits until his interest passes and he is on to something else before putting them away again. The parents try to minimize their use of words like "no" and "don't" and use distraction and positive incentives in their place. In this kind of home environment the Dabakis children have the freedom to explore; their feelings of capability and self-esteem are allowed to grow.

Create a Home Environment with Love and Warmth, But Also an Expectation of Success

Let your children know that they are loved for themselves—not for their accomplishments or how their behavior reflects upon their parents. Make allowances for their shortcomings and failures, but at the same time make it clear to them that you see them as competent and able individuals. In this kind of environment your children will learn that it is OK to venture forth, to take risks, and that when they do, on occasion, fail at something they attempt it is not the end of the world. As you see them as competent, and as they see themselves as successful, feelings of self-esteem will be maintained and enhanced.

It's not enough just to tell your child he's great and you love him. You should also encourage him to enjoy experiencing new things. You can teach him to expect to succeed and to keep trying when things get tough. You need to teach him skills so that he can be great at something and know it. Though we might expect children to work at some things just because we think they are important—piano lessons for example—most of their motivation should be personal. The things we would like our children to succeed at may be quite different from the things they deem important. As they get older more and more of their effort and accomplishment should be based on their own goals rather than upon our desires for them. Success should be measured in terms of how well they can succeed in ways that allow expression of their own genuine feelings—their own creativity and individuality—not by how well they achieve the things that are important to us.

An Example of Courage and Accomplishment*

A young man had a strong desire to succeed in baseball. As a child he was clumsy and awkward; yet he became one of the greatest ballplayers of all time. In his early years he was shy and easily hurt, and was not outstanding at anything. He was small for his age and considered not too bright. Other boys threw rocks at him and called him names. Because he couldn't either bat or catch the ball very well, no one wanted him on their team. But he was persistent because above all else he wanted to play baseball. With his strong willpower and long hours of practice he began to improve and eventually to excel, until he became one of the greatest first basemen ever to play the game. He had many injuries and illnesses, but sick or well he never missed a

*Taken from *Lou Gehrig: An American Hero*, by Paul Gallico.

game. Even late in his career, unable to straighten up because of lumbago, he still got his share of hits. Once he was knocked unconscious by a wild pitch and suffered a concussion. But he played the next day and got four hits. Near the end of his playing days his hands were X-rayed, and the doctors found that he had broken every finger on both hands, some twice, but never mentioned it to anyone. The amazing thing was that through all the pain of breaks, sprains, pulled and torn tendons, muscles, and ligaments, he played as well as ever. When he began to fail rapidly because of a degenerative disease, he worked even harder so as not to be "a handicap to his team." He was Lou Gehrig, a name never to be forgotten by fans of baseball.

With our help our children may be able to duplicate in part the accomplishments of a Lou Gehrig. While life is not always easy, there is joy in overcoming. Our children must be willing to risk failure in order to experience success. With this success comes increased feelings of competency and self-esteem, and they, and we, can truly "sleep when the wind blows."

CHAPTER 6

Help Your Child to Be Bold and Assertive

Virtue is bold, and goodness never fearful.
                              —Shakespeare

A very important ingredient of self-esteem is the approval of peers. As a child perceives that he is valued by his classmates, he comes to value himself accordingly. The qualities that children admire in one another vary, of course, according to age. But at almost any age confidence and assertiveness are prime qualities in effective social adjustment. A child who is retiring and unsure of himself is likely to be an underachiever; he is also apt to be overlooked and undervalued by both adults and peers.

Through the years there have been many studies of the qualities most important to the popularity and self-esteem of elementary schoolchildren. Surprisingly, the more popular children are not necessarily those most free of obnoxious traits; neither are unpopular children necessarily free of good traits. The thing that seems to be most important at that age level is assertiveness—the ability to make an active impression of some type on the group. As a child finds himself able to make such an impression on other children, and as they respond to him in positive ways, his self-confidence and self-esteem are magnified.

It is important to distinguish between assertiveness and aggressiveness. When one is assertive he behaves in a positive way with confidence. Force, compulsion, and ill manners are aspects of aggressiveness, not assertiveness. The type of assertive behavior that I am recommending is guided by ethical standards and concern for others as well as oneself. While the assertive person does not allow others to take unfair advantage, neither does he exercise compulsion over others.

Helping Children to Be Assertive

There seems little doubt that some children have an easier time becoming bold and assertive than others. Some of this potential seems to be built in, and may even come from innate or inherited qualities. Nonetheless, there are things that parents can do to help children be more assertive. Here are a few:

1. Set a good example of assertiveness. I know a man who has struggled all his life to be more self-confident and assertive. He told me about his father, whom he refers to as a "wonderful man," and describes as an outstanding husband and father. The one ingredient that seems to have been lacking is assertiveness. This man has a clear memory of going shopping with his father and seeing him stand back a little at the counter as people who came in later crowded ahead to be served first. Often, when this would happen, he would say, "Dad, we were here first!" and his father would respond with a comment like, "It doesn't really matter, son, we're not in any big hurry." This was only one example of

his father's tendency to put others ahead of himself. Now, as an adult, this man finds himself doing the same kind of thing—standing back when he really should be assertive.

It would be nice if everyone were socially sensitive, and thoughtful and respectful of others. But, alas, such is not the case. Some people will continually push, demand, take advantage as long as there is someone who will let them. Those who fail to resist their rudeness become victims. Proper assertiveness does not require fighting, arguing, or other obnoxious behavior. Often it only requires a quiet comment. In the case of the man who let others crowd ahead, all he would need to have said was, "I'm sorry, but I believe I was here first." Almost all people would stand back and say, "Oh, I'm sorry." The man would then feel better about himself, and his son would have a positive example of appropriate assertiveness.

Some people find it impossible to be assertive until they become angry. If they are mad enough the self-restraint vanishes. The trouble with this is that rationality and good manners may also vanish. The assertiveness that should have been exerted in a quiet, calm fashion gets out of control, and when the person "comes to himself" later he is likely to feel rather foolish.

A parent who wishes to model assertive behavior should accept responsibility for requests and expectations for the child. It would not do for a father to say, "Your mother doesn't like you to do it that way." Or the mother should not say, "Your father wants you to..." Say, "*I* want you to...," and then state the expectation clearly.

2. Teach your child to say "no" to inappropriate requests. Sometimes children give in to others in order to be well thought of. I know a teenage boy who does many things with friends that he does not really enjoy just to be accepted as one of the group. And then he complains to his family about it, saying that the activity was "dumb," and he

wished he had just stayed home in the first place. It would make sense for him to try to make friends with peers who share his interests.

There are some potential dangers in teaching our children to be adventuresome and willing to take risks. They may experiment with mind-altering substances or engage in antisocial activities for thrills. But the child or adolescent who has strong self-esteem and whose parents have instilled basic values is less likely to become involved, and when he does is less likely to continue beyond the initial experimentation period.

Sometimes a child will do things that not only does he not enjoy, but which also violate his own values or sense of right and wrong, because someone else wants him to do it. The inappropriate request or demand may come either from another child or from an adult. Some cases of child molestation and sexual abuse could have been prevented had the child realized that he had the right to resist adult requests that violate his personal rights. Boys and girls should know that no one, even a parent, should touch them in the personal areas of their bodies, which can be described to them as the part that is covered by their underwear or a swimming suit. Nor should anyone display these parts of the body to them.

Pre-adolescent and adolescent children need similar instruction in areas of alcohol, drugs, and sexual experimentation. There are organized programs available to teach them to just say ''no''! Sometimes children go along with things they would rather not do for fear of being different or not being accepted by others. Through such programs a child who may not have had the courage to resist on his own can find the group support that he needs. A child who is assertive may not need such group support in order to resist pressures to succumb.

Parents can help children to explore alternatives to potentially harmful situations in advance so they are not caught off guard when the problem arises. As children are able to meet each situation successfully, and maintain personal values, they are also able to protect themselves from self-demeaning labels and lowered self-esteem.

3. Teach your child to stand up to bullying. A bully usually picks on children younger or weaker than he out of personal feelings of inferiority and inadequacy. He judges that the other child will avoid him, run away, or not fight back, and the feeling of dominance over the other child bolsters up a sagging ego. I learned a valuable lesson as a child of about 12 when, after suffering from scorn and threats of such a bully for several months, "valor became the greater part of discretion," and I stood my ground, fully expecting to get beat up. To my great surprise my opponent backed down, and my role changed from victim to victor. I still have a strong recollection of the feeling of relief and satisfaction that that incident provided.

There is a temptation when hearing that one's child is being bullied to step in and try to solve the problem and protect the child. But almost always it is a mistake to do so. In fact it is more likely to exacerbate the problem rather than to help it. The bully may make your child's life even more difficult. And when two parents become involved, each one is inclined to believe and take the side of his own child. It is much better for your child to solve the problem on his own. Let him know that boldness is almost always the proper response to a bully. Even if he does take advantage of his greater age or size and prevails over your child, your child will be the winner in increased respect for standing up to the bully, from those who observe, often from the bully himself, and certainly in terms of the child's own self-respect.

Though the advice to let your child fight his own battles is usually correct, there are times, of course, when you must intercede. There are bullies who are sadistic, severely maladjusted, psychopathic or even psychotic. Their parents may be unwilling or unable to restrain their boorish and dangerous behavior. I am not suggesting that a parent should stand by and let a child be physically manhandled and brutally beaten. Sometimes it is necessary to complain to the parents or to a law enforcement officer, or even to initiate legal action against a person who is unfairly abusing your child.

4. Teach your child the posture and body language that will command respect from others. Much communication takes place in ways other than words. A child who slouches or walks around looking at the ground, and who never looks anyone in the eye, is not apt to engender much respect or self-respect. One of the favorite bits of advice of George W. Crane, a psychologist who wrote a nationally syndicated column some years ago was: "Go through the proper *motions* and you will soon begin to feel the corresponding *emotions*." Children can be taught to use appropriate body language and posture, and as this becomes a habit, good feelings about themselves will be a by-product. But a note of caution—these things must be taught in a positive way! Nagging and scolding are counterproductive and demeaning; as a child feels bad about himself, and unable to please his parents, his posture is more likely to get worse.

5. Teach skills to your child. While I would resist the idea that every child needs to have boxing and/or karate lessons, it is probably safe to say that many children can derive satisfaction and a boost to self-assertiveness through the development of physical skills. A child who lacks any strong talent for athletics can improve in assertiveness with other talents such as art, music, drama, and debate. In a sports dominated society such as ours, such talents are often short-changed. But logic would dictate that these other areas are at least as important to ultimate life success as sports. A child who finds he can do things that are of significance to

himself and others in any area of endeavor is in a good position to develop feelings of capability and confidence which make it easier to be assertive.

6. Help your child to cope with anxiety in a productive way. James Collier, author of "Anxiety: Challenge by Another Name," published in the *Reader's Digest*, told how as a young college student he had a chance to work on a ranch in Argentina, owned by his roommate's father. He worried about being so far away from home, about the language and customs, and about other things, and found himself waking up nights in a sweat. So he passed up the opportunity. He was sorry when another friend was asked and accepted the roommate's offer, and found himself later feeling low as he unpacked cartons at the local supermarket. He felt even worse when he went back to college in the fall and discovered that the roommate and his friend had had a wonderful time. He says that at that time he developed a rule for himself: "Do what makes you anxious; don't do what makes you depressed." Collier further explains that he is not talking about severe states of anxiety or depression that require medical attention. He is talking about the kind of anxiety we call stage fright, butterflies in the stomach, a case of nerves, and the kind of depression that we call "the blues," when we can't get going and are low in interest and energy.

Our children face this type of anxiety often as they try to develop a new skill, such as riding a bicycle, or go out for the team or the school play. Many children back down from attempting such things when they find them too scary. And that's when they need our encouragement and support. Collier says that a corollary to his basic rule is: "You never eliminate anxiety by avoiding the things that caused it." New and different things are almost by definition scary, but our children have to be taught, and to really believe, that you can't learn if you don't try. They also need to learn that as they persist in scary things, the fear will be lessened or eliminated altogether. As they learn not to turn away from things that seem to involve some risk, their experiences will broaden, they will usually be successful, and self-confidence and self-esteem will get a big boost.

7. Teach your child to be bold. Arthur Gordon, in his delightful book, *A Touch of Wonder*, recounts a time when he faced a decision that seemed to involve considerable risk, and sought advice from a friend older and wiser than himself. The friend scribbled on a piece of paper ten words which Gordon says constitute the best advice anyone ever gave him: "Be bold, and mighty forces will come to your aid." Gordon suggests that there is nothing vague or mysterious about these "mighty forces." They are latent powers that we all possess: energy, skill, sound judgment, creative ideas, and physical strength and endurance. We often possess more of these attributes than we realize.

It seems clear that the mighty forces that come to one's aid are psychic in nature. But, as far as the outcome is concerned, it does not matter whether they come from a benevolent providence or represent a galvanization of forces from deep within the individual. In either case it is clear that people are sometimes able to perform tasks in an emergency situation that they are not able to perform at another time. Such instances are well documented. Consider the case of the woman who, when faced with a ferocious looking dog, baring his teeth, growling, and dragging a chain, was able to climb a tree to avoid the possibility of being bitten. Later, when she looked at the tree again, she was quite astonished that she had been able to climb it.

It was reported in a syndicated newspaper article that a five-year-old boy saved his six-year-old sister's life, using the Heimlich maneuver. When he saw her beginning to choke, he got behind her and picked her up from the floor, though she was bigger than he, grasping her around the waist. The mother, at first, tried to shoo him away, thinking he would only aggravate the situation, but he persisted, and the food particle was expelled from her mouth. Later, when asked how he knew what to do, the boy said that he had seen this maneuver demonstrated on television. What an example of a child acting with boldness when the situation required it!

When we teach our children to be bold we are not exhorting them to be reckless or foolhardy. Boldness means that from time to time we make deliberate decisions to attempt things that we are not sure that we can really do—we risk failure. But isn't it better of us and our children to aim high and occasionally fail than to shrink with timidness from trying? A famous mountain climber once said that sometimes a climber will deliberately get himself into a position where he can't back down, he can only go up. If there is no way to go but up, then you *will* go up! We don't all need to climb physical mountains, but most of us at times in our lives need to meet and conquer "psychological mountains" that stand in our way.

"Be bold, and mighty forces will come to your aid." What a motto for a person, or a family, to take on as a guide. Make a sign with these words and put it up on the family room wall, or tape it to the refrigerator. Repeat it to your children on appropriate occasions, and help them to really believe it. As your children learn to behave boldly—not brashly, not impetuously, not rudely, but boldly—the whole world will open up for them; their self-confidence and self-esteem will grow by leaps and bounds.

CHAPTER 7

Let Children Make
Their Own Decisions

**There are two good things in life, freedom
of thought and freedom of action.**
                    —W. Somerset Maugham

In my work as a psychological consultant in the schools, I often am in a position to mediate difficulties between adolescents and their parents. One such case involved a fifteen-year-old girl. The referral came directly from the mother, which is somewhat unusual. More often it is a teacher or school administrator who is concerned about a child's academic progress or emotional or social adjustment. As I talked to the principal and to the girl's teachers prior to meeting with the mother, I found them to be surprised that this particular girl had been referred. They reported that she was a good student, was attractive, and appeared to be liked by her peers. Next I talked with the girl herself, and found her to be pleasant and friendly, but a bit lacking in self-confidence. The only problem she reported was that her mother treated her "like a baby." Then I met with the girl's mother. She appeared to be an intelligent and articulate woman, and as I talked with her it was clear that she loved her daughter and wanted the best for her. But she talked about her as though she were about ten years old instead of fifteen. This was her youngest child, the "baby" of the family, and it was obvious that she was growing up faster than the mother wanted her to. The main concern of the mother was that her daughter was "rebellious," and seemed to resent any parental directive.

I tried this approach in working with the mother: First I asked her to think about any events she could recall that had happened about five years previously, and she did. Then I asked her if it seemed very long ago that these things had happened, and she said no. Then I reminded her that in just such a short time in the future her daughter could be married or otherwise on her own—sooner if she chose to go away to college. I suggested that it would be easier for her, and her daughter, to adjust to the separation if it were to take place gradually rather than all of a sudden, and that perhaps now was the time to give her daughter "some of her own air to breathe"—to let the reins go just a little so that the girl would be more able to make it on her own when that time came. This approach seemed to provide the breakthrough that the mother needed to see that she was trying to nurture too much and not allow her daughter to make enough of her own decisions. When we brought the daughter into the conversation on the mother's next visit, I was able to set up a "contract" in which mother and daughter made some agreements and some compromises which both could accept. Because this was basically a good mother-daughter relationship, with love on both sides, the problems were resolved rather quickly, and relatively easily.

Children's Decisions vs. Parents' Decisions

It is not uncommon for parents to make too many decisions for their children, but to do so is to foster dependency and low self-esteem. Few parents do this deliberately; it's just that when they are with their children every day, as the child gradually matures, they may not always recognize the move to a new stage and the need to deal with situations differently.

Parents may have the best of intentions when they make decisions for their children, hoping to keep them from making any mistakes. But even if this were possible, would it be a good thing to do? Obviously not! Though mistakes may be annoying, inconvenient, and sometimes costly, they provide children with the opportunity to learn from experience and make better choices next time.

How can a parent know which decisions should be made for children, and which decisions should be left to them? An important guiding principle is that children should not be allowed to make decisions in which irresponsible choices have potentially dangerous consequences to themselves or to others. Obviously, a three-year-old should not be allowed to choose whether or not to play out in a busy street. A fifteen-year-old girl should not have the option of deciding to move into her own apartment. In situations where a wrong choice has a potential physical, psychological, or moral danger, it is the parent who must make the decision.

My wife and I were visiting friends one Sunday afternoon when the phone rang and their nine-year-old daughter answered it. In a few minutes she came into the living room and asked her parents if she could go ice-skating at a local rink with two of her friends. As background, I need to mention that in this family Sunday is regarded as a time for attending church, visiting with friends or relatives, visiting the sick or shut-ins, resting, listening to good music, etc. Commercial entertainment on Sunday is discouraged in the church they attend. The mother reminded her that it was Sunday, but told her she could decide for herself whether or not to go—that she was old enough now to make such decisions herself. The mother's answer seemed to take the girl aback. She probably expected the mother to say, "Dear, you know it's Sunday; of course you can't go." She sat thinking for a few minutes; then went back into the other room to call the friend to say she could not go.

Let's analyze this situation a little further. First of all, I believe that in this case the mother was not "playing games." She was not saying, "You decide, but you had darn well better decide the way *I* want you to." The decision was really the child's to make, and had she decided differently nothing further would have been said; there would have been no recriminations. The choice was not serious enough in the parent's view as to pose any real problem or danger, and so the daughter was allowed to decide for herself.

Suppose that the mother had proceeded under the assumption that the decision was hers to make rather than the daughter's. What if she had simply told the girl she *could* go skating? The daughter knew before she asked what the parents' attitude about Sunday activities were. Had they said "yes" she would have probably been confused and wondered why they had abandoned their values so readily. What if the parents had said "no," as the daughter had anticipated. She may have simply accepted the decision; in fact, she may have wanted them to say "no" so she could have an easy "out" with her friend. But, especially if the relationship with parents was not good, it could give her the ammunition she needed to argue, cajole, or become emotional in order to gain attention or set up a power struggle. The approach that the mother used of allowing her daughter to decide neither contributed toward overdependency nor rebelliousness. By placing the responsibility for the decision upon the girl, where it belonged, Mother sent a message to daughter that she regarded her as intelligent and responsible enough to decide for herself—giving a boost to her feelings of capability and self-esteem.

It is difficult to stand by and watch children make choices that we know are not as good as those we would make for them. But they need the practice of making decisions for themselves, and of living with the consequences of those decisions. A good question to ask ourselves frequently is, "What difference will it make?" If there is not a significant danger to the child or to others, and if the advantage of promoting the child's autonomy outweighs the inconvenience or other potential problems, the decision should be left to the child.

The Transition from Parental Control to Self-Control

The shift for a child from having parents make all or most of the decisions to making all or most of his own decisions should be a gradual one. We need to allow our children choices that are appropriate to their ages. An infant, obviously, has no capability to make decisions, and everything must be done for him. By late adolescence or early adulthood, children should be almost entirely responsible for their own behavior and make almost all of their own decisions. The transition from complete helplessness to almost complete autonomy should be made gradually as children grow and mature and become capable of more and more logical decision making. Let's take a look at the kinds of choices parents should permit at each stage of childhood.

1. The Toddler and Preschool-Age Child. Very early in life parents should present options for their children which allow them to make decisions and satisfy their growing need for autonomy. As they are allowed to choose for themselves,

feelings of capability and self-esteem have a greater chance to blossom than if everything is decided for them. Of course the choices that are offered toddlers and young children must be very simple ones. A basic rule is to never allow children to make decisions that a parent can't live with. Often parents violate this rule by asking a two- or three-year-old child questions such as, "Should we go to bed now?" or "Do you want to come and eat now?" And of course the most natural and truthful answer the child can give is often "No!" Then the parent may try to coax, or subdue the child by force. How much better it would have been for the parent to say simply, "It's time for dinner," or "It's bedtime," and then pick the child up or take his hand and lead him to the table or bedroom.

Choices that are given to toddlers and preschool children should be those that make little or no difference to the parent: "Do you want to wear your red or your yellow pajamas?" "Should I read you a story, or do you want to listen to your record player?" "Do you want to drink your juice out of your cup or a regular glass?" If on a particular day you don't really care whether your child plays inside or out, you can give him a choice. But if you need a little time for yourself, don't say, "Tommy, do you want to go outside and play?" (He may, after all, say "No." During the negativistic age, children will say no even to things they want to do just to exercise their autonomy.) Just help him on with his coat, say, "I want you to play outside for a while," and gently push him out the door (assuming, of course, there is adequate supervision, a protected area, or that the child is old enough to stay out of danger).

2. The Elementary School-Age Child. As children become old enough to attend school, the decisions they make have more importance and meaning. But the principle remains the same: You only give them the opportunity to make decisions in situations where you will support them regardless of

which way they decide. At this age parents can help by teaching good decision-making skills. If we make a decision for a child we may help him past an immediate situation, but if we teach him to make wise decisions for himself we prepare him for life.

One way of teaching decision-making skills is to explore alternatives with our children. We can use questions such as, "What would happen if you...?" "If he does that again, what will you do?" "What are some ways you could handle that differently next time?" "If you did that, how do you think you would feel afterward?" "Let's write down some things you could do next time this happens, and then decide which ways are best." We should let the ideas come from our children and refrain from providing them with pat solutions of our own.

Probably the best way to help children develop decision-making skills is by example. We can be a good model by being decisive. If they see us vacillating, either in personal decisions or in what we allow them to do, they may learn to be poor decision makers too.

Parents frequently ask my advice about giving children an allowance. One of the advantages of doing so is that it offers them practice in decisions that involve spending money. Age seven or eight is a good time to begin to give an allowance. Give a modest amount at first, and then increase it as children get older. Continue to give an allowance until they are old enough to earn their own money. Children should have considerable freedom to decide how to use their money. While it may be quite appropriate to suggest that a portion be saved for a worthwhile purpose, the rest can be spent in any way they wish. If they spend it foolishly they may learn to be more careful next time. It is far better for children to learn by mistakes when they are young and the amount of money wasted is small than to learn the same lesson when they are older and the results are more serious.

Parents often ask whether the allowance should be given in exchange for work done around the house or whether it should be given to them whether they earn it or not. While arguments can be given either way, I feel that there is something to be said for making the allowance unconditional; in a family everyone helps, and also in a family everyone shares the family income. If the allowance is contingent upon work, children may decide to forgo the reward and not do the work. So parents who want to teach the children to share in the responsibility of maintaining the home might do well not to tie work tasks to the allowance. It may be a good idea to provide optional work opportunities for pay in addition to the required work. Earning money and learning how to use it wisely can contribute greatly to feelings of capability and enhance self-esteem.

3. The Adolescent. Eloise had just graduated from high school and was planning to start college in the fall. She wanted to buy some new clothes for school, and because she had had a part-time job for two years she was able to finance most of the cost herself. She would like to have gone with her friends to shop for the clothes, but her mother felt that where so much money was involved she should personally help Eloise decide which clothes to buy. She was so persuasive that her daughter ended up buying mostly clothes that her mother liked and felt were appropriate. Was Mother right in involving herself so actively in clothes selection for Eloise? Certainly there would be nothing wrong in going to the store or offering suggestions upon request. But for her to take the prime role in deciding what to buy was wrong, especially since her daughter's earnings were paying for most of the purchases. By the end of high school a child should be able to decide pretty much what clothes to buy and wear. If Eloise is a normal young lady she is likely to resent her mother's inflicting her choices upon her; and some of the clothes are likely to hang in the closet unliked and unworn.

By the time children reach the teenage years the decisions they are called upon to make will be of importance. Moral choices emerge at this stage of life. If parents have well-formulated values and make it clear that certain things in life are very important, and if their children adopt these same values, decisions become simpler to make. They may be almost automatic. As children grow older they may reject some of their parent's cherished values and make different decisions than parents would make; but they have been given a starting point. Even though they temporarily reject the values they have been taught, they will often return to them later in life. But if parents have not taught clear-cut values there is nothing for their children to return to, and they may have great difficulty in formulating values of their own.

For some people moral and ethical values are appropriately taught within the framework of an organized religion. Others choose to teach values in their own way, independent of a religious orientation. Moral instruction can come in many forms. In any case it is good for children to develop a sense of continuity, an understanding of things greater than themselves. Occasionally one hears a parent say, ''I don't believe in forcing my values on my children or pressuring them to believe the way I do. I'll let them learn about all different philosophies of life, and when they get old enough they can decide for themselves what they want to believe.'' This kind of attitude teaches children that moral values are not very important. Parents should teach the values they believe in to their children, by word and by example, realizing that they have the right to modify them in their own ways as they become older and grow toward responsible adulthood.

Parents do not have the right to make crucial long-term decisions for children. Martin's father runs a dry-cleaning business that has been in the family for three generations. Martin is the only boy in the family, and the father has always assumed that eventually he will take over and run the business. He has never talked to his son about any other vocational possibility; indeed, it may have never entered his mind that Martin might not be delighted about the prospect of moving into a lucrative and well-established business. But Martin, who has worked in his father's establishment on Saturdays and after school, is sick of the sights, sounds, and smell of dry-cleaning. He wants to be an electrical engineer. On the few occasions when he has broached the subject with his father the conversation has gone nowhere. The father thinks it is a fine idea for Martin to go to college. In fact, he has always regretted that he did not have an education himself. But he views college for Martin as a valuable social experience, not as vocational preparation.

A parent in a profession or business would do well to refrain from putting pressure upon a child to follow in his footsteps. If he is happy and successful and enthusiastic about his work there is every chance that his son will elect the same profession. But if the child elects to pursue a quite different field, that should be his prerogative.

Sometimes a father or mother puts pressure upon a child to do something that he or she didn't do. Mr. Lindon had to drop out of medical school for financial reasons, and now he is convinced that his son Marc should be a doctor. A parent has no right to expect a child to fulfill vicariously his own unfulfilled dream.

Another very important area of decision making is friendship, dating, and marriage. It is difficult for a parent to stand by and see children form alliances with friends who have traits or behaviors that they do not approve of. But after they reach a certain age there is little effect you can, or should, exert on the friendships that are established. Your best hope is that you have taught your children a good set of values. If they identify with you and internalize your values, they will usually choose friends who exemplify those values, and when they don't the relationships tend to be transitory.

Adolescents are especially apt to resent attempts to choose their friends for them. It is not a good idea for us to forbid them to associate with particular friends since they are likely to resent our interference and go ahead and see them anyway. If children feel a need to rebel against parental authority, an excellent way to do so is to deliberately associate with friends to whom parents object. We should invite our teenagers to bring all of their friends to the house and be friendly with them. As we get to know them better we may find that our objections are unfounded. In any case, having the young people in our home rather than off in some unknown area gives us more control over the kinds of activities that take place. If a friend has traits or characteristics that are in opposition to the values that our children have grown up with, they are apt to be able to perceive them more clearly against the backdrop of the home environment, and some of the luster may be lost from the relationship.

While what I have said about children and adolescents being allowed to choose their own friends is generally true, there are, of course, exceptions that need to be made. In rare cases your child may establish a relationship with someone who has such a serious personality or character disorder that the potential danger from such an association is too great to be ignored. If your child will not respond to reasonable persuasion to discontinue the relationship, strong action must be taken for their own protection—perhaps even some type of legal action to keep them apart.

In the long run, the confidence we show in our children's judgment and in their ability to choose appropriate friends will increase their self-confidence and strengthen our relationships with them. As we help our children at each age and each new stage of development to make appropriate decisions for themselves, we contribute toward their feelings of capability and self-worth.

CHAPTER 8

Spend Quality Time with Your Children

> **The greatest of all sacrifices ... is the sacrifice of time.**
>
> *—Plutarch*

Harold and Doris Bradford want to enjoy life while they are still young. Their life is a continual round of dinner parties, shows, and other engagements. Harold is a young business executive and Doris is a buyer for a department store chain. They have two children, a boy, 10, and a girl, 8, who are cared for most of the time by a housekeeper. The children have the benefit of music lessons, dancing lessons, and a variety of other activities. But they see little of their parents. When the children are involved in a recital or a school program the Bradfords are usually conspicuous by their absence, since they are usually too busy to keep track of their children's activities. The Bradford children have everything except the thing that is most important—time with their parents.

One of the few gifts that parents can give that is of real

and lasting importance is the gift of themselves. Parents who plan ahead and put forth special effort to be with their children communicate to the children that they are important and that parents value their association, giving a boost to their feelings of self-worth. Good parenting requires that we spend time with our children. Ideally, each child in a family should have individual time every day with each parent. This time may be difficult to arrange, especially in a large family, but the desirable benefits are well worth the effort.

Involve Young Children in Your Own Activities

A father may say, "I realize that I'm not spending the time I should with Mark. But it's all I can do to just get done the things that need to be done. Where am I going to find the time to spend alone with Mark?" But it's not always necessary to create extra time; you can involve children in things you would be doing anyway. Young children love to go to the store, the bank, the post office, or most any place the parent will take them. It provides an excellent opportunity to get to know a child better and find out what thoughts occupy his attention. It also provides a chance for your child to learn more about you.

As a child gets older, going to the store with Mom or Dad loses its appeal. He will usually elect to be with friends rather than with parents or other family members. Though parents are sometimes threatened by this choice of peers over them, it is a normal and healthy stage in a child's development. But being with parents is still important. Now is the time to develop some mutual interests, whether it be hunting or fishing, ball games, shopping trips, movies, or whatever appeals to both you and the child. As parents and adolescents participate in mutually enjoyable activities they can interact as friends and get to know each other as people, relatively free from the dominant-subservient relationship that has existed heretofore. Interacting as equals in the types of activities mentioned will not undermine a parent's effectiveness in situations that require exercising of parental attention. In fact the good relationship that has been built will make it easier for the child to accept the logical requests and demands that are placed upon him.

Find Time to Interact with Your Children

Mr. and Mrs. Parkinson pride themselves upon the fact that in fifteen years of parenting they have seldom left any of their three children with baby sitters. On the rare occasions they have both been away from home and from the children in the evening at the same time, either Mrs. Parkinson's mother or sister have usually been available to sit with the children. Night after night Mr. Parkinson works in his shop and Mrs. Parkinson busies herself with household duties. Even at the evening meal it is unusual for all family members to be there at the same time, and everyone seems to be always in a hurry. It is a rare occasion when the family has a leisurely meal with good conversation among family members.

It has often been said the quality of time that a parent spends with a child is more important than the quantity. While there is some truth to this statement, there are some problems with it as well. For one thing, "quality time" is hard to define. For a young child, just being with the parent, even when she is engaged in routine household activities and some interaction takes place, is valuable time spent. Another problem with the concept of "quality time" is that it can be a way for a parent to salve her conscience about spending too little time with a child. An occasional ten minute "enrichment period" with a parent is not likely to meet a child's need. The presence of adults and older children in the home at the same time does not guarantee that any significant interaction is taking place. A parent whose face is in the paper, or who is transfixed by the events that are taking place on the television set, may be as inaccessible to a child as if he were out of town.

Mr. Chang is an executive in a large corporation. He finds that he must often work about 60 hours a week to meet his company's expectations. But, in spite of these heavy demands, he does not allow his work to interfere with his home and family. His practice is to never bring work home from the office. He may not arrive until after seven some evenings, but when he is home he is really home. His attaché case remains at the office. When one of his children is in a piano recital, a ball game, a play, or a school program, he is there. He would like to be able to relax in front of the television set more often, but realizes that this is one pleasure he must limit severely if he is to have time to devote to his wife and children. He is never too busy to listen.

Much of the time that you spend with Your children should be mutually enjoyable. If you are grudging of the time and keep looking at your watch and thinking about the more "important" things you should be doing, your children will sense that you are with them just out of a sense of duty, and the experience will be much less likely to build self-esteem. But if you really enjoy the time you spend with your children they will feel lovable and wanted, and feelings of self-worth will be enhanced.

Helping with Homework

Mrs. Madsen is a caring mother who likes to be helpful to her children by assisting with homework. Recently her daughter Joan was assigned by her English teacher to write an original poem. When Joan mentioned the assignment to her mother, Mrs. Madsen took right over and decided what the poem should be about, and then helped her to write each line. Joan's teacher was quite impressed and had her read the poem to the class. How did Joan feel about this recognition? Instead of a feeling of elation and pride, she felt some uneasiness and feelings of guilt. She realized that the poem was much more a creative effort of her mother than of herself. The lack of faith that her mother had in her ability to write her own poem lowered her feelings of capability and self-esteem.

Parents should be willing to provide appropriate help when their children really need it. But it is important to be careful not to assume responsibility for a child's homework or make it their own production rather than the child's.

Another thing to be careful about when helping children with homework is to remain calm and patient. It is often easier to be patient with someone else's child than with your own. If you find yourself becoming impatient or anxious and hear an "edge" in your voice, or if you feel "put upon" by having to help, it would be much better to withdraw from the situation and let someone else provide the help the child needs, if in fact he really needs help at all. Sometimes children display inadequacy to gain sympathy and keep the parent involved. This may be either conscious or unconscious on the child's part. To feed into this display of inadequacy is to reinforce your child's feelings of helplessness and lower self-esteem.

Time spent by parents for instructional help should be for short intervals. With young children ten-minute sessions are often long enough. The activities should be as enjoyable as possible to minimize resistance and help sustain interest and attention. If you have a home computer there is an abundance of programs available which present learning activities in the form of games, and a child will often proceed on his own for long periods of time because of the intrinsic appeal that such programs provide.

Use Bedtime Effectively

For many children bedtime is not a particularly enjoyable or sought-after time of day. Some of the reasons are quite obvious. A young child may resent having to go to bed earlier than older siblings; not only may it seem unfair, but it also means "leaving the field" to his rivals. He may not feel tired, or he may resent having to leave an enjoyable activity right in the middle of it. He may even be going through a stage in which his bedroom holds certain fears. The shadows in his room may cause some concern, or he may imagine that there is a monster in his closet. For these and other reasons bedtime is a good time for a child to receive parental support, and it provides a significant opportunity for parents and children to interact in positive ways.

You can lessen your child's aversion for going to bed by providing a quiet enjoyable interval with him. You might take turns and spend 15 minutes every other night with each child while the other parent takes time with a different child or performs needed household activities. Bedtime should be a quiet peaceful time in which the child can "wind down" from a busy day. Reading bedtime stories, listening to the child read, playing a quiet game, singing songs, or simply discussing the events of the day can all create a good atmosphere for sleep and help to build good parent–child relationships in which self-esteem can flourish.

Teach Your Child to Share You with Others

Your child must understand that he cannot always monopolize your time—that there are others to whom you also owe allegiance. Parents should not be so concerned about spending time with their children that they have little or no time to spend with each other. Strong husband–wife relationships are important and need to be cultivated. A child who enjoys individual time with each parent should be willing to allow brothers and sisters the same opportunity.

Relationships outside the home are also important. While children should not be neglected, and parents should not indulge their recreational needs at a child's expense, parents have both the need and the right to associate with other adults and maintain appropriate relationships in a variety of settings.

Spend Time Together as a Family

Not only is it important for parents to spend individual time with children, but it is also important to spend time together as a family. Family activities and traditions can boost morale and contribute to self-esteem of family members. Family solidarity develops as parents and children work and play together. Time spent together can build family pride.

Ruldolph Dreikurs, a well-known child psychiatrist and author of *Children: The Challenge*, suggests that the family council is one of the most important ways of dealing with troublesome problems in a democratic way. This is a meeting, preferably scheduled for a definite time on a definite day each week, in which problems are discussed and solutions sought. In such a meeting it is important that each member has a chance to be heard and to bring up any problem he desires. Then all family members work together to try to solve the problem, and the majority opinion is upheld. It is not a family council meeting if the parents are the only ones who present problems and solutions; all children in the family should be stimulated to give their input. Neither should parents dominate and overrule the group decisions that are made. Chairmanship can be rotated so that children learn to conduct a meeting, thus enhancing their feelings of capability and self-worth.

Many families have found such a council meeting to be beneficial in building family solidarity and enhancing self-esteem in family members. The meeting's effectiveness can be enhanced by having regular treats or by following it with enjoyable games and activities.

CHAPTER 9

Discipline Your Child Effectively

> **Train up a child in the way he should go: and
> when he is old, he will not depart from it.**
> —*Proverbs 22:6*

From the time Marcie was born her parents have given her an abundance of freedom. They do not feel it fair to impose their wills upon her; nor do they wish to dampen her spirit or curtail her initiative and creativity. Now, at age fifteen, Marcie is the envy of her friends because she is a law unto herself. She goes where she wishes, does whatever she wants to do, and says whatever she feels like saying. It appears that in no way is she accountable to her parents. The parents see their role as one of providing a good home and the comforts of life; they do not exert any effective discipline.

Contrast Marcie with Mindy, who is the same age and lives nearby. Mindy's parents, especially the mother, are very controlling. They want to know where she is at any given moment. If she is 15 minutes late when returning from school, she must give an accounting of her time. If the mother sees her at the front doorstep talking with a friend, she later wants to know what they were talking about. She is seldom allowed out of the house in the evening without one or both parents accompanying her. Both Mom and Dad keep close tabs on her friends of both sexes. In short, while Marcie is given little attention or supervision, Mindy is stifled by it.

Marcie appears happy with her freedom—glad that she does not have to get parental approval for the things she does. She boasts to her friends, and teases them about being dependent on, and controlled by, their parents. But secretly she is not as happy as she pretends. She interprets the lack of parental discipline as a lack of caring, and says to herself, "Why don't Mom and Dad *make* me do what I should do. If they really loved me they would care what happens to me."

Mindy interprets her parents' control as a lack of trust and a feeling that she is incapable of governing her life properly. Further, their overly strict discipline makes her insecure about her parents' caring for her.

Coming from such different homes, what do Marcie and Mindy have in common? Both are very low in self-esteem. Extremes in parental discipline of either permissiveness or autocracy affect a child's self-concept adversely.

Parents Who Allow Too Much Freedom

Parents who are too permissive may act out of a number of motives. They may fear losing their children's love if they are too strict. They may worry about the correct approach to take to a problem and be so afraid of doing the wrong thing that they do nothing. They may be so caught up in their own affairs that they do not know, or perhaps even care, what the child is doing. Or, like Marcie's parents, they may mistakenly think that a "hands off" approach is the way to raise happy and well-adjusted children. But whatever the reason, children are apt to interpret a lack of discipline as a lack of love and caring.

Overly permissive parents do children no favor. Parents need to provide logical, consistent and fair behavior controls for children until they are old enough and mature enough to develop internal controls. Raising children is a bit like growing a garden. What would we think of a person who planted seed and then said, "I'm going to let my garden grow in its own natural way. I don't believe in cultivating it. I don't thin my carrots because it doesn't seem fair to uproot all those tiny carrots and let them die. And besides, I'm really too busy anyway. And I won't bother to water the garden—I'll just let the rain take care of it." A garden grown under this philosophy will not be impressive either in its appearance or in its productivity. Neither is it likely that a child who has been allowed to "grow like Topsy" will be impressive to others or high in accomplishment or self-esteem. Effective parental discipline is essential to the development of a healthy, well-adjusted child.

Children Need and Want Limits

An important role for parents is to set clear and reasonable limits for their children. In an autocratic home the limits are more narrow; parents decide what behavior is appropriate for their children, and then enforce that behavior. In a democratic home children are allowed more freedom; they are also allowed to express their feelings without recrimination. Psychologically healthy and well-adjusted children can come from either kind of home, though children from more democratic homes tend to develop more initiative and creativity.

The type of home that tends to be most ineffective is the

laissez-faire one. "Laissez-faire" in French literally means "to let do." This type of home pushes the concept of democratic leadership too far. It is fine for parents to allow children free expression, but to give over the reins of leadership to them is to start them on a runaway ride that is uncomfortable for both child and parent; who knows how far the out-of-control carriage will go until it eventually overturns?

A laissez-faire leadership in the school is as ineffective as in the home. John Dewey's so-called "progressive education" of a generation ago had points to recommend it. However, sometimes it went too far in giving the children the responsibility to decide on classroom activities and what was to be learned. Children feel insecure and uncomfortable when rules and limits are unspecified. This is typified by the child in a "progressive" classroom who asked, "Mrs. Johnson, do we have to do what we want to do today?"

Sometimes a child like Marcie will continually "test the limits" by making behavior progressively more objectionable. They seem to be asking themselves, "How far do I have to go before somebody stops me?" The worse the behavior, the more likely it is that feelings of guilt and worthlessness will develop. The misbehaving child is almost always a child with low self-esteem.

Parents Who Control Too Much

At the other extreme of parents who are too permissive are Mindy's father and mother, who provide more limits than the child really needs. People who themselves were raised in a home where parents were overly strict and controlling tend to become the same kind of parents. They rely too much on punishment to get children to do what they want them to do. When I talk about punishment I am referring not just to physical punishment such as spanking, but to any type of adverse consequence we place upon a child in an attempt to get him to do something we want him to do, or to refrain from doing something we do not want him to do. Alternatives to spanking might be sending a child to his room, "grounding," or withdrawal of privileges. Though punishment may appear to be an excellent way to enforce correct behavior, unless it is applied very wisely it can have many negative consequences and impair the child's feelings of self-worth in a number of ways. For one thing, punishment creates hostile and resentful feelings, which are likely to be directed toward the punishing agent rather than toward the behavior that brought on the punishment. Rewards for behaving correctly, on the other hand, are more likely to create positive feelings. The punished child is apt to feel guilty or inferior, mitigating against feelings of self-worth; the rewarded child receives a psychological boost of self-esteem.

Another reason that punishment is often ineffective is that it fails to provide direction for the child's behavior: It says, "Stop that!" But it does not say what to do instead. Reward, on the other hand, does provide direction for the child. Since the desired behavior is followed by a "payoff," which can be anything from praise to a tangible reward, the child is likely to repeat it in order to be rewarded again.

Parents are told to punish the behavior—not the child. Let him know that it is not him you dislike, but whatever the act was that occasioned the punishment. Unfortunately, this is often easier to say than to do. The punished child often feels demeaned and helpless against the larger, all-powerful parent.

Consider this example: Mother is washing dishes and through the kitchen window sees Dale, age 6, and his younger brother Paul, age 4, playing together in the backyard. Suddenly, there is an eruption of emotion, and she is horrified to see Dale knock "sweet little Paul" down and then sit on him, holding his arms to the ground. Quickly she removes her apron and runs out the door to solve the problem and settle things. On her way she breaks off a branch to use as a switch. When she reaches the "scene of the crime," she begins to apply the switch to an appropriate spot, crying loudly, "I saw what you did to Paul! I'll teach you to pick on your brother." Mother doesn't realize just how appropriate her words are. That is exactly what she *is* doing—teaching him to pick on his brother, but not when Mom is watching. There is something incongruous about punishing a child by doing the same thing to him that he is being punished for doing. The lesson she is inadvertently teaching is that it's OK to hit someone if you are the one in charge and are old enough and strong enough.

Unless you are a rare parent you will not be able to avoid punishing your children altogether, desirable as that might be. It is not always possible to find a positive way to correct behavior. We should not feel guilty if we resort to punishment on occasion, if the punishment is not unduly severe. But when, instead of punishing children for doing what we don't want them to do, we are able to reward them for doing what we do want them to do, we will see positive results in both behavior and self-esteem.

An Alternative to Punishment

Often discipline is equated with punishment. When a father says, "I'm going to have to discipline my son," he may mean, "I'm going to have to punish my son." But, as we have pointed out, punishment is only one part of discipline, and not one of the best methods at that. The old adage, "You can catch more flies with honey than with vinegar" certainly applies to raising children. Rudolph Dreikurs, one of America's best-known child psychiatrists, has written an excellent book, *Children: The Challenge*. In it he suggests that parents learn to replace punishment with the use of natural or logical consequences. If Max doesn't come home at the agreed upon time, he misses his dinner. If Tammy forgets to take her completed homework assignment back to school, she suffers whatever consequence the teacher imposes.

One problem with the use of consequences is that the natural consequence of the child's behavior may affect the parents more than it does him. Or the consequence may be so potentially damaging to the child that it must be prevented at all costs. Then parents must substitute a logical consequence—something that the child will recognize as coming about as a result of his own behavior rather than being externally imposed. If Tom, age 5, insists on running out into the street, he is taken home and not allowed to go outside for the rest of the day. Mother might say, "When you forget and go out into the street I'm so afraid you might be hit by a car. Play inside today, and we'll see if you can remember better tomorrow." This statement makes Mother's action a logical consequence. If she has said, "Tom, you naughty boy! You know you're not allowed to play out in the street. Get in this house and don't go out again for the rest of the day!" her action would be perceived as punishment.

Another example: If Mark fails to complete an assigned task, he has to miss the movie that other members of the family attend. Again, the way the parent handles the situation can make it either a punishment or a logical consequence. If the father says, "Mark, I warned you that if you didn't get the job done you couldn't go to the show," it is a punishment imposed on him by the father, and the connection between the omission and the result is not clear. If, on the other hand, the father were to say, "Mark, there just isn't time for you to finish that job before we have to leave for the movie. I feel bad that you're going to have to miss it,"

he would be using a logical consequence. Mark misses the
movie because he chose to procrastinate.

The advantages of using natural or logical consequences
instead of punishment are clear. Hostility toward the parent
is avoided because outcomes emerge directly from the
child's behavior rather than being imposed by the authority
figure. With punishment the parent is in an adversary role
with the child, and there may be scolding, shouting, ill-will,
and sometimes physical pain—all detrimental to the child's
self-esteem. In the use of natural or logical consequences
the parent can remain friendly and sympathetic, and be on
the child's side, expressing sincere regret that things happened
as they did. And feelings of self-worth are maintained.

Let's illustrate the use of a logical consequence with a
common situation with which many readers can identify.
Carlos, age 14, loved to play basketball with his friends
after school. His boundless enthusiasm and youthful energy
kept him from tiring, and he would often play for hours and
lose all track of time. It was not uncommon for him to
arrive home after the rest of the family had finished dinner.
This behavior was annoying to his mother as she had to
either keep the food warm in the oven or get it out again and
warm it. Constant reminders that dinner was served prompt-
ly at 5:30 P.M. had no effect. What course of action could
the mother take to correct her son's behavior? She could use
punishment by "grounding" him or making him miss supper.
She could nag and scold, hoping that it would eventually
pay off. But instead she decided to use logical consequences.
The next time Carlos was not there at dinner time
she served the rest of the family, and the kitchen was
cleaned up and everything put away when he finally arrived
home. When he asked about supper she told him in a
matter-of-fact way that he was welcome to get it out of the
fridge and warm it provided he left the kitchen as he had
found it. After a few repetitions, including one in which he

found that no one had saved him a piece of his favorite pie, he began to watch the time and was able to appear regularly at the dinner table.

A good way to apply logical consequences in a home setting is to use a chart. Are there some regular tasks you want your children to perform, or some behavior you want to help them correct? Continual reminders can turn into nagging and scolding, which can damage the parent–child relationship and demean the child. A chart on the wall can objectify the situation and obviate the need for such reminders.

As I consult in the public schools, I find that many parents are unable to get children to perform the tasks assigned to them. I often suggest that they try using a chart, and perhaps we will make up one together. I suggest that they keep it simple and just work on a few things at a time. Otherwise the child feels overwhelmed, and the whole effort becomes counterproductive. To make things equitable, and to avoid singling the child out for special attention, the chart may include the names of all the children in the family, with activities and tasks appropriate to each age. With young children, stickers or gold stars can be used to indicate the completion of a job each day. Older children are more likely to respond to check marks, and they can be allowed to fill them in as they complete the task. At the end of a prescribed period of time, perhaps a week, there should be some type of "payoff." With very young children a week will be too long to have to anticipate; with adolescents a longer time frame might be used. The reward does not have to always be something material; in this busy world a little extra time with Mom or Dad might be effective.

Often when I suggest setting up rewards to shape a child's behavior, a parent will say, "I don't believe in bribing my children." Then I explain that offering an inducement to a child for something he should be doing is not bribing. We all work for rewards of one kind or another every day. "Bribing" is giving someone a payoff for something they *shouldn't* be doing.

Some families have a rule that when all of the children fill in all of the spaces on the chart they have a fun family activity, such as bowling, horseback riding, swimming, or any number of other choices. Many parents have been amazed at how the child's behavior has changed without any nagging or scolding, or sometimes even reminding. If a fun family activity is at stake, parents can bet that children will remind each other of tasks or behaviors on the chart. What happens when one child does not cooperate and the rest do? It depends on the situation. If he has had full opportunity to earn the chance to go, and chooses not to comply, it would not be appropriate for the parents to let him go along anyway. If the child wishes another chance, and the other children are willing to postpone the activity for a few days, that decision would be fine. The point is that it is appropriate at times for parents to use external incentives in guiding childrens' behavior.

Make Children Responsible for Themselves

There is a temptation to protect children too much from some of the natural consequences of their behavior. Here is an actual example: Brent is a sound sleeper, and it has always been hard for him to get himself up in the morning. Knowing this, and not wanting him to be late for school, his parents go into his room each morning to wake him—not just once, but several times. As a high school senior he still expects this service from his parents. He and they are convinced that without their intervention he would be late to school every day.

Let's evaluate Brent's "wake-up service." Doesn't he have wonderful parents to be so concerned about him and make certain that he is never late for school? Though the parents may see themselves as helpful and nurturing, they are taking on a responsibility that should belong to Brent, and in the process they are teaching habits of indolence and feelings of helplessness. Years ago they should have given Brent a loud alarm clock and expected him to get up at the appropriate time by himself, and allowed him to face whatever consequences resulted from oversleeping. Just one or two late mornings might have taught him to get up on his own.

If we become slaves to our children and are always there to protect them from themselves, we tend to make them too dependent upon us. If a child has to miss lunch no serious harm will result, and he will be much less likely to forget it again. If he does not have a book that is needed at school he may suffer some mildly unpleasant consequences that help to jog the memory next time. If our children have to stand on their own feet and be responsible for their own behavior, they learn to be more responsible people, and feelings of capability and self-esteem are enhanced.

Be Consistent

Inconsistency works against effective discipline perhaps more strongly than any other aspect of parent–child relationships. Children can tolerate an autocratic home environment in which the limits are clear and consistent. They know what to expect and can avoid difficulty by staying within the limits. While a democratic home is thought to be the ideal, an autocratic home is usually more conducive to feelings of security than is a home that is too permissive or one where the limits are unclear or constantly changing.

Almost any virtue can be pushed to such an extreme as to become a vice. Consistency in an extreme form can become rigidity. While parents should not be arbitrary or capricious in their leadership, children need to learn that situations change; unexpected and unpredictable events arise. Children need to understand that unforeseen events may require a modification of plans on occasion.

Support Each Other; Work as a Team

Children should not be allowed to play one parent against the other. Here is a familiar example:

"Mom," said fourteen-year-old Carla, "a bunch of us are going to the midnight movie and then sleep out in Jackie's backyard." "Oh dear, I don't think that's such a good idea. You've been up late several times lately, and I don't think you're getting enough sleep." "Oh, please, Mom! The whole gang is going, and I've been wanting to see this show for such a long time." "I'd really rather you didn't go. Ask your father and see what he says."

"Dad, can I go to the late movie and then stay over at Jackie's house?" "You'd better ask your mother." "I did, and she said to ask you." "Well, tell her if she thinks it's OK, then it's OK with me."

"Mom, I talked to Dad, and he thinks it's OK for me to go." At this point Mom is likely to feel some irritation and resentment toward Dad. Lacking the ability to say "no" and mean it, she relied upon Dad to play the "heavy" role. Each parent is leaving it to the other to make the decision, and Carla is able to manipulate the situation to her advantage. In this situation the parents should have communicated with each other directly and arrived at a joint decision.

It is unlikely that a husband and wife will agree one hundred percent of the time with regard to the proper action to be taken; but it is important to present a united front. If our spouse should on a given occasion handle a situation differently from the way we would have handled it, we should refrain from being critical or taking issue in the child's presence. It would be especially unwise for one parent to countermand the decision the other parent has already made. Support the decision, even if it be wrong, and then talk it over quietly in private later. Parents who quietly and consistently support one another and work together are good models for children. Such parents are likely to build the type of secure home in which self-esteem can flourish.

CHAPTER 10

Treat Your Child with Courtesy and Consideration

> The basis of good manners is self-reliance.
> Those who are not self-possessed obtrude, and
> pain us.
>
> —*Emerson*

Dale Carnegie tells of a conversation he once had with Charles Schwab, one of the first American businessmen ever to be paid over a million dollars a year. This was in the days when there was no income tax and a person who made fifty dollars a week was considered to be well-off. Yet the newly formed United States Steel Company was willing to pay Schwab, as its president, over three thousand dollars a day. It was not because he was a genius or knew more about making steel than others. Rather, as he told Carnegie, it was because of his ability to deal with people. He said, "I consider my ability to arouse enthusiasm among my people the greatest asset I possess, and the way to develop the best that is in a person is by appreciation and encouragement. There is nothing else that so kills the ambitions of a person as criticism from superiors. I never criticize anyone. . . . If I like anything, I am hearty in my appreciation and lavish in my praise.''

The same principles that Schwab recommends in dealing with employees can serve parents well. Too much criticism from parents can indeed kill the ambitions of children, cause bad feelings, and lower self-esteem. Unfortunately, the tendency of many teachers and parents is to give the child a great deal of critical attention when he is doing the wrong thing and to give no attention when he is behaving correctly. And we really should learn to do just the opposite. Praise and positive attention contribute strongly to the child's feelings of lovability, capability, and self-worth.

Sometimes we hear people talk about putting on their best manners with people they deem important. But if good manners are necessary in dealing with people outside the home, why not equally indispensable when dealing with our own family matters? No one should be more important to us than our own children. And as we treat them with courtesy and consideration we convey to them that they are important.

We teach manners in the home much more by example than by anything we say. Our children need to learn the simple rules of courtesy that are so important in all human relationships. It begins by learning to say ''please'' and ''thank you,'' but there is much more than this that is involved. They need to have respect for other people's needs and opinions; and they will learn to respect others largely by how well we treat *them* with such respect.

A Poor Example

Maurine and Joe are the parents of three children, ages ten, eight, and five. Both parents are quite stern, and their children have to learn to walk a straight line. Joe, once a

Marine sergeant, barks out orders to his children in much the same fashion that he used to direct the men under his command. Maurine, though polite to husband and friends, does not treat her children with the same courtesy and consideration, and words like "please" and "thank you" are seldom used. When working in the kitchen she shoulders aside any child that is in her way without the usual "pardon me" that might be expected.

How can Maurine and Joe expect their children to learn to be respectful and use good manners unless they model this behavior for them? Is it likely that children will treat each other with courtesy and consideration when they are not treated this way by parents? Children should not be allowed to be rude to parents or to other adults, but neither should they be exposed to rudeness.

A Good Example

George and Ann Page make courtesy and consideration prime values in their home. They would not think of entering a child's room without knocking first, nor would they ever consider reading letters or diaries without the child's knowledge and permission. Children in the family are taught not to borrow clothing or other possessions without asking, or even look in a closet or drawer that is not their own without permission.

You could visit in the Page home for weeks and never hear or see an example of bad manners. Words like "thank you," "you're welcome," and "please" are just as common there as in any other setting. Is it any wonder that strong feelings of love and harmony exist in this home, or that family members have strong feelings of self-esteem?

Using good manners with children and treating them with respect is the best way to help them to develop the same traits. Good manners are foreign and artificial to a child who has not grown up with them; they come as natural as breathing to a child that has experienced them in the home.

We do not, after all, own our children; they are entrusted to our care for only a few short years. While we need to exercise adult leadership, in some areas of life children need to be treated as equals if they are to develop self-esteem.

Avoid Sarcasm, Ridicule, Nagging, and Scolding

The parent who resorts to ridicule and sarcasm when dealing with children acts out of anger and hostility, coupled with feelings of helplessness. He or she lacks the skill to approach the child in a more positive fashion. Sarcasm and ridicule can have far-reaching and devastating effects upon self-esteem. Consider comments such as these:

"You stupid idiot! You ought to know you'd ruin your new pants if you played football in them."

"That's your third piece of cake. You already look like a blimp. I think it's disgusting that you don't have any control over your appetite."

"Can't you ever say anything that makes any sense?"

"You really know how to dress. That red blouse and purple scarf really set off your red hair. Now all you need is an orange skirt to go with it."

"You little monster! Come over here so I can knock you into next week!"

Do parents really talk like that to their children? Unfortunately, some do. Can you imagine how strongly such comments work against self-esteem?

Equally undesirable are such comments made about the child in his presence:

"This kid is so dumb he doesn't know enough to scratch

where it itches." (How many times will the boy have to hear this in order to learn that he is "dumb"?)

"George has his father's stubbornness; there's no sense in even trying to reason with him." (If George didn't already have his father's stubbornness, he would surely develop it by hearing himself so labeled time and again.)

"Look at this kid! Did you ever see anybody so clumsy? He was born with two left feet." (We can be fairly sure that the boy in question will become increasingly clumsy as he hears these comments.)

Needless to say, parents should not talk to or about children in these ways. Such comments are destructive of self-esteem. But they should also avoid extreme statements such as, "My Dan is the smartest boy in the whole school!" or "Joannie is pretty enough to be a movie star!" or "Tom is the most popular boy in town." Though it may seem on the surface that these comments would enhance self-esteem, as the child realizes he can't possibly live up to such laudatory descriptions there may be a reverse effect, contributing to feelings of failure rather than to high self-regard.

Teach Your Child to Interreact with Adults Appropriately

A generation or two ago it was common to think that "children should be seen but not heard," or perhaps even "children should be neither seen nor heard." When a person not well known to the family was visiting it was common for children to stay in another room, perhaps peeking around the corner to see what was going on. Fortunately, this does not happen as much today; in fact, some families have shifted over to the other extreme in which children are allowed to dominate the scene and prevent adults from carrying on a sustained conversation. Either approach is to be regretted. Children need to learn to interact with adults appropriately. This is a good way for them to learn to feel comfortable with different people and develop good social skills.

In a group situation in which there are both children and adults, the children should be treated as "people" just the same as the adults. Consider this situation: Nancy and Marie go on a shopping trip together, and Marie takes along her ten-year-old daughter, Ann. Most of the time Marie and Nancy carry on an animated conversation about adult topics. They never draw Ann into the conversation, or talk about anything she would understand or relate to. Her mother occasionally asks her to hurry, or to stay with them and not get lost, but that is all the verbal interaction that takes place between the child and the adults. Nancy and Marie would never treat another adult like they treated Ann, and if they did they would certainly offend her with such rudeness.

Contrast the above situation with this one: Mrs. Torrance seems to feel that the reason for her existence is to serve her children. She waits on them constantly—makes their beds; cleans up after them; and does not risk offending them by imposing requirements or standing in the way of anything they wish to do. If she is talking to a friend or neighbor and one of her little darlings runs up and interrupts the conversation, she will stop in the middle of a sentence and turn her complete attention to the child.

Though it is important to treat children with courtesy and consideration, it is possible to carry consideration too far. A child deserves the same privileges as other people—not more. We must be willing to serve our children, yet guard against becoming their servants. Children who learn to expect special favors and believe that they are not bound by the rules that govern others have a rude awakening when they have to face the "real world." As they have difficulty in social relationships and find themselves unable to control peers and teachers, self-esteem may plummet.

Somewhere there is a happy medium between ignoring children and making ourselves slaves to them. A child should not be treated as either a nonentity or as the center of the universe, but as a valued and respected member of the group.

Avoid Embarrassing Your Child

Embarrassment mitigates against self-esteem. A very poor time to correct a child is when there are others around, especially friends. It can be demeaning for the child and self-defeating for the parent. Put yourself in the place of a child who, with one or more friends present, hears from a parent such comments as these:

"Wise up, and don't act so stupid!"

"Andy, how come you were the very last one to finish the race? Try harder next time!"

"Look how nice Vera looks. Why are you always dressed so sloppily?"

"Candace, I'm surprised at your report card—three C's, two B's, and only one A. Pam, let me see your report card; I'll bet you did a lot better."

If you were a child hearing such references to yourself, would you be spurred on to greater heights of achievement and more acceptable behavior? Possibly, but not too likely! It would be ideal if we could make all of our interaction with children happy. Most of us, being human, scold them on occasion. But we can avoid sarcasm and ridicule, and we can focus on their behavior rather than their character. And we can correct them quietly, away from friends and other family members.

Don't Expect Too Much

One of the classics of American journalism, by W. Livingstone Larned, is called "Father Forgets." It appeared originally in a publication called the *People's Home Journal*, and was later reprinted in hundreds of magazines and newspapers throughout the country. The father steals into his small son's room as the boy is sleeping and speaks to him as though he were awake and as though he could understand. As he sat reading his paper in the library he began to feel guilt and remorse for the scolding and criticism he had dealt out to the little boy a number of times during the day for such things as not washing his hands or cleaning his shoes properly; throwing his clothes on the floor; gulping his food, spilling things, putting his elbows on the table, and putting butter too thick on his toast while at breakfast. The enumeration of criticisms continued through the afternoon and evening. He remembered that as he was reading, the son came in timidly, and hesitated at the door. Glancing up from the paper and impatient at the interruption, he had snapped, "What is it you want?" Without saying anything, the boy ran across the room, threw his arms around his father's neck and kissed him, and then ran up the stairs. It was shortly afterward that the paper slipped from his hands, and a sick fear came over him as he began to realize the habits he was developing of finding fault, of reprimanding, of expecting too much. And, as he kneels at the child's bedside, ashamed, he resolves to look at the little boy's many fine qualities, to bite his tongue when he begins to criticize, to have fun and laugh with him, to be a real father, and above all to say to himself again and again, "He is only a boy—a little boy! I have asked too much, too much." Before we condemn and criticize our children, let's try to understand them. Let's try to step out of the autocratic and adversary role that parents too frequently adopt with children, and see our children as real people, not as though they were our possessions. Wouldn't it be wonderful to be able to say, along with Charles Schwab, "I never criticize [my children]. If I like anything, I am hearty in my appreciation and lavish in my praise"?

Contrast the way you treat your best friend with the way you treat your children. If you are like some parents you may find a real difference. As one mother said, "If I treated my best friend like I treat my kids, she wouldn't be my best friend for long. In fact, she wouldn't be my friend period!" The parent-child relationship precludes our being friends with our children in the usual sense of the term, and some people make themselves look ridiculous in the attempt to be accepted on the child's level. We need to be a parent rather than a friend, and our children share a very different experience with peers than with us. However, in another sense, our children should really be our friends; and if we treat them with the same consideration we treat our best friends there is a good chance that they will come to think of us as their friends too!

CHAPTER 11

Deal Effectively with Unpleasant Emotions

> I count him braver who overcomes his desires
> than him who conquers his enemies; for the
> hardest victory is the victory over self.
>
> —*Aristotle*

"Daddy, I don't want to ride the pony!"

"Oh, don't be silly, Jack. Of course you want to ride the pony. Come on now, let me boost you up here."

"Daddy, Daddy, no! Please don't put me on the pony. I'm scared."

"Scared! Don't be silly, Jack. The pony won't hurt you. What's there to be afraid of?"

Father still persists in trying to set Jack, who is now stiff as a board, upon the pony's back. At this point Mother intervenes. "Max, you can see he's scared to death. Let the boy alone."

"Donna, I lost two good hours of work by leaving the office early, and look at the time and money we've wasted. Besides, no son of mine is going to be a sissy!"

Father's attempt to talk his son out of his fear of the pony was predictably unsuccessful. Children have only limited ability to reason, and even less when under emotional stress. How might the father have approached this situation? It would have been much better for him to have recognized the fear and said, "It's a little scary, isn't it? Why don't we just watch for a while." After watching other children ride, the father might have let the boy feed the pony an apple and pet it. If, after that preparation, the little boy is still reluctant to ride, it would be best to abandon the attempt and try again at another time.

Most of us find it easy to handle our children's happy emotions. It's gratifying to laugh with them, share their excitement with new experiences, or hug them and tell them we love them. But their more difficult emotions often leave us puzzled, embarrassed, angry, or insecure. One thing that will help is to realize that the more unpleasant emotional feelings are just as normal as the pleasant ones. Our job as parents is not to squelch them but to help the child express them in ways that are socially acceptable and that will maintain feelings of self-worth.

The Need for Unpleasant Feelings

Wouldn't it be wonderful if we could spare our children and ourselves all unhappy, unpleasant emotions? Shouldn't we eliminate all fear, anger, sadness, loneliness, embarrassment and jealousy from their lives and promote only love, happiness, and other satisfying emotions? We obviously do not have the power to eliminate bad feelings from our children's lives, and fortunately so. Ideal as it sounds, those feelings are important not only to the quality of life but also to its very preservation. Can you imagine the fate of a child who knew no fear or no anger? How long could such a person survive? And how could one really appreciate the happy emotions without having the bad ones for a comparison.

No, our job as parents is not to smooth the way entirely for our children or protect them from all unpleasantness. On the other hand, we do need to protect them from undue emotional stress. Children should not be expected to shoulder adult emotional burdens. Our main job as parents is to teach them constructive ways to handle their emotions.

How Do Emotions Relate to Self-Esteem?

Self-Esteem = Feelings of Capability + Feelings of Lovability. It would be hard to overstate the importance of this formula. Emotional states that contribute to these feelings of being lovable and capable promote self-esteem; emotional states that detract from them weaken self-esteem. A child who is not in control of his emotions is not apt to feel either lovable or capable. A child who is angry is not very lovable, and knows it. A child who is fearful may feel helpless in dealing with life situations. The emotion of jealousy involves love, fear, and anger. There is fear that he is losing love, and anger at whoever is perceived as the cause of this loss. The threat of losing love has deleterious effects upon a child's self-esteem.

Helping Children Deal with Unpleasant Feelings

There is much we can do to help children to be more in control of their emotions. As we are able to do so we will help them to be happier and more productive. Here are a few suggestions:

1. Be casual about bad feelings and realize they are normal. Parents need to be careful not to overreact to their

children's emotional outbursts, and by all means not to lose emotional control themselves. Do not embarrass or ridicule your child because of his emotions. Ridicule and embarrassment are notoriously poor ways of changing behavior, but all too effective ways of contributing to low self-esteem.

2. Set a good example of emotional control. It would be very hard for a parent who lacks emotional control to teach it. "Do as I say, and not as I do," is ineffective advice. A child does not learn good emotional control from a parent who resorts to childish behavior, lashes out verbally or physically, says cruel things to get even, or uses other hurtful ways of responding to bad feelings.

When your child is angry he may say or do things that make you angry in return. But avoid the temptation to retaliate. Talk quietly and calmly, and try not to raise your voice. Do not let yourself be drawn into a power struggle. In the heat of battle it is easy to say things that will be regretted. Should you impulsively say something or do something that you regret, do not be afraid to admit your error and apologize to the child. He will feel more respect for you, not less, when you honestly admit a mistake. When it is your child who makes the impulsive statement, avoid recriminations. If he says it under his breath it may be well to pretend not to have heard it. If he says it openly, accept the feeling calmly, and realize that he too has a right to hurt feelings.

But some people exercise too much control over their emotions. They believe they should never let a child see them sad, angry, or fearful. A child raised by such parents may feel guilty when he experiences difficult emotions himself. It's all right for children to know that parents are people too—that they have all the human emotions. A recognition that you have normal fears and experience anger at times need not impair your effectiveness as a parent. But of course they need to see you handling these emotions well and in control.

3. Let your child "own his own feelings." This is a concept developed by Thomas Gordon, author of the well-known Parent Effectiveness Training (PET) program. If your child in the heat of emotion says, "I hate you," how should you respond? Should you cry and say, "How can you say such a naughty thing and make Mommy feel so bad?" Should you say, "You ungrateful little brat! Well, I hate you too!" Should you spank him, or wash his mouth out with soap? Or should you try to talk him out of his feelings by a comment such as, "Oh, you couldn't hate your very own mother!" At the moment he really feels the hatred, and probably the best thing to do would be to remain calm and either say nothing or make some comment such as "You're really mad at me, aren't you?" Almost before you know it your child will have forgotten that he was ever angry and will be coming to you for a cookie or a hug.

Too often parents try to talk children out of their feelings with statements such as, "Oh, big boys like you are not afraid of the dark!" "You don't really hate your sister!" It would be much better to accept the feeling in a nonjudgmental way: "Yes, the dark basement is a little scary, isn't it?" "Sometimes even people we love do bad things and make us feel we don't like them." It's good for your child to know that in growing up it's OK to feel anger, hate, or jealousy at times, though we need to control the expression of these feelings.

It is important not to punish children for their unpleasant feelings. If and when punishment is indicated, it should be for bad behavior, not for an honest expression of a bad feeling.

It is common for parents and teachers to force children to apologize and say they are sorry when they really aren't: "Now go and give Karen a hug and tell her you're sorry for saying such a naughty thing!'' Help your child to recognize his error so the apology is sincere and voluntary. Forced apologies are meaningless and cause resentment in a child.

4. Help your child find socially acceptable outlets for bad feelings. If your child responds inappropriately when he is upset, it is up to you to help him to learn to behave in a more acceptable way. This is not a time for punishment. One good thing to do is to encourage him to talk about how he feels; talking itself can often reduce tension.

Physical activity can also sometimes help to dissipate bad feelings. This may be a good time to get the sidewalks shoveled, the lawns mowed, or the garden spaded. One of the advantages of competitive sports is that they can provide a healthy and socially acceptable outlet for emotional feelings.

Sometimes when a child is very angry at his little brother or sister it may help to say something like this: ''I know you are real mad at Tony, but I can't let you pound on him like that. Why don't you punch the punching bag; if you want, you can pretend it's Tony.''

It is important for your children to have some type of emotional outlet. Repressed emotions not only cause psychological distress but they also can have harmful physical consequences as well in the form of stomach ulcers and other health problems.

5. Look for the cause of the emotional reaction. Occasionally the reason for a child's emotional distress is not immediately evident. Three-year-old Bobby's parents were puzzled at the fear that he had of the barber, a friendly man who had a good way with children. They did not know of any bad experience the child had had in a barbershop. Then suddenly the answer came. Bobby was associating the barber's white smock with a doctor's uniform. He had had an illness which required medical treatment and separation from parents for several days; now he feared a repetition of that frightening event.

Dad couldn't understand the reaction of Joshua to his simple request to go down in the cellar and bring up some apples. He became angry and asked why he was the only one in the family that ever did anything, and why couldn't Max go? What Dad didn't know, and perhaps even Joshua, himself, was that he was afraid of the dark, damp cellar, with its possible monster, or at least spiders. Yet he felt that he was too old to have such fears, and would be embarrassed to let Dad know that a big eight-year-old boy was afraid of that silly old basement. The emotion of anger was more acceptable to his feelings of capability and self-esteem than the emotion of fear would have been. Knowing the cause for an emotional reaction can often give us an idea of how best to approach it.

6. Help your child to have more control over his environment. Parley, age three, was frightened by the sound of the vacuum cleaner. His mother found that if she let him be the one to turn it on and off so the sound did not catch him off guard he was no longer fearful. Randy was afraid to go to bed and imagined that there were monsters lurking in the shadows of the bedroom. His father solved the problem by giving Randy a new flashlight to keep right by his pillow, so that when he began to be frightened he could reassure himself that there were no monsters after all.

Feelings of anger can also sometimes be prevented by helping a child to have more control over his environment. Anger is often caused by frustration, and if we can help to avoid needless frustration, we can help the child to maintain composure and control and feel better about himself. A child who is in control of his life is likely to develop self-confidence and self-esteem. Of course we are not suggesting that all frustration be removed from a child's life. It is by facing up to and conquering small frustrations when young that a child is prepared to cope with more serious and basic frustrations later on.

In 1929, a psychologist by the name of John B. Watson wrote a book called *Psychological Care of Infant and Child*. We have learned much about children since 1929, and some of the advice in this early book is naive and ill-advised. One of his suggestions was that parents provide a fenced-in backyard and then dig many holes for the child to crawl in and out of like an obstacle course, "thus learning to cope with adversity almost from the moment of birth." Certainly it is not necessary for us to deliberately set up frustrating situations for our children; life itself provides more than enough frustration. While we may wish it were possible to spare our children all frustrating, anger-provoking situations, allowing them to work through their own problems develops feelings of competence and self-esteem.

7. Use negative adaptation to control mild fears. Sometimes the best way to help a child to overcome a fear is to force him to face up to the feared situation until he loses his fear of it. This is called "negative adaptation." Negative adaptation is recommended when the fear is a mild one. An example would be the young child who is afraid of riding the elevator. If the parents takes him on the elevator anyway, providing whatever emotional support the child needs, the fear will usually disappear in a very short time.

If a child has a mild school phobia, the best solution is for the parent to take him to school anyway, insisting in a matter-of-fact way that school is where children belong. She might even point out that it is against the law for him not to attend. She may also want to see if there are some specific things at school that are fear-provoking for the child so that some intervention can be made by the teacher. In the case of a severe school phobia, where the child is actually in a state of panic, negative adaptation is not the answer. The child is probably in need of more help than the parents can give, and professional assistance should be sought from the school psychologist or from a private practitioner.

8. Use conditioning to help your child overcome fear. John B. Watson, the psychologist mentioned previously, deliberately conditioned Albert, a nine-month-old infant, to fear a white rat. He did this by associating the sight of the rat with a loud gong. Prior to this time neither the rat nor objects that might be associated with it (white cotton, a white beard, other small animals) were frightening to Albert. But when a loud noise was made just at the time Albert was shown the rat, and this was repeated a number of times, the sight of the rat alone caused a strong fear response. Furthermore the fear then spread to the objects mentioned above that resembled a rat in some way.

It may seem very cruel to deliberately condition fear in a child. Certainly they learn enough fears without our help. In fairness to Watson let it be said that he did not leave Albert in this fear-ridden condition. He reconditioned him so that the fear was overcome altogether. This was done by presenting the rat at a distance several times, always when the child was happy and engaging in pleasant activities. Gradually he brought the rat closer and closer, always under positive circumstances, until it could be placed right on Albert's lap with no sign of fear.

No responsible and caring parents would deliberately instill fear into a child. However, life itself provides many fear conditioning situations, such as the child who learns to fear the cellar because of its association with darkness, the child who fears the teacher because he has a loud voice, or the child who fears going to sleep because he associates sleep with death. You can recondition the child to overcome fears such as this. For example, in the case of the fear of the cellar you might do a series of very fun activities with the child in the cellar until it is associated with pleasant things rather than with darkness.

9. Withdraw from emotional situations when appropriate. Sometimes the best thing to do when your child is experi-

encing an unpleasant emotion, such as anger, is to quietly remove yourself from the scene. If your young child should throw a temper tantrum, the best thing to do generally is to simply walk out of the room and busy yourself in another part of the house. Few children are able to maintain a temper tantrum without an audience. Poor ways to handle the situation would be to punish the child for the tantrum or to try to talk him out of it. Such approaches only intensify the emotion, or teach him that poor behavior is a good way to get attention from adults.

10. Use a time-out procedure when appropriate. The time-out technique can be used effectively both at home and at school for children who are angry and out of control. It consists of removing the child from the situation to provide a cooling off period. This removal should be done as quietly and inconspicuously as possible to avoid other embarrassment or undue attention for the child. Ideally, the child should not see the removal as a punishment, but as a chance for him to rest and regain self-control. A parent who says, "Get out of my sight, you little monster. You're mean and nasty and don't deserve to associate with normal human beings!" is not using your time-out method. The proper approach is for the parent to say something like this: "You're really upset. You need time to cool down and get yourself under control."

The time-out procedure should be used only for short periods, and the younger the child the shorter the time should be—perhaps only a matter of minutes in some cases. Sending a child to his room for the entire day is not an effective way of using time out.

One of the problems in using time out is the lack of availability of a good room. Ideally the room should have four blank walls, and be free of any interesting things to play with. Otherwise time out may be a reward to the child, and he may misbehave deliberately in order to repeat the experience. If you send him to a room where there are books to read, a comfortable bed on which to relax, and perhaps even a stereo sound system or television set, you may defeat the intent of the time-out technique.

11. Reduce jealousy in your home by giving each child his share of attention. An infant demands a great deal of attention because of his helplessness. But you should not give this attention at the expense of older siblings. At the advent of a baby the toddler psychologically requires more attention—not less. A mother might ask, "But how can I give extra attention to my toddler when my new baby requires almost all my time? I'm only human, and there are only so many hours in a day!" But much attention can be given to the toddler without spending extra time. As the infant nurses at the mother's breast, instead of constantly cooing and commenting about how sweet, beautiful, and wonderful the baby is, the mother would do well to notice and talk to the young child who is standing by watching. This is a good time for the father to play a more active role, either doing things with the older child while the mother cares for the baby, or freeing the mother to spend time with the older child by caring for the infant himself.

It is wise for a visitor to a home where there is a new baby and a toddler or preschooler to give some attention to the older child. Picture this situation: a group of adults gathered around the baby's crib, making the kind of sounds that infants bring out in adults, while four-year-old Tommy stands in the corner watching. A perceptive and understanding adult would break free from the group and come over and talk to Tommy. A visitor who brings a baby present would be wise to bring some small item for Tommy; it would not need to be at all expensive; a small toy or lollipop is enough.

A mother can also give the older child attention and make him feel a part of the situation by asking him to help her in ways that are appropriate to his age. Even a very young child can help Mommy by bringing her the baby's rattle, taking the baby's shoes or socks off, or shaking the baby powder on after the baby's bath. A mother should refer to the infant as ''our baby'' instead of ''my baby.'' Some mothers help their young children to feel a part of things by giving them a doll and letting them feed, bathe, or dress ''their baby'' at the same time Mother cares for the real baby.

CHAPTER 12

Communicate Effectively with Your Child

Parents spend the first part of a child's life getting him to walk and talk, and the rest of his childhood getting him to sit down and shut up.

—Jacob M. Brande

Why are children, especially teenagers, so hard to understand? Why do they flout our moral standards and traditions? Why can't they just accept the fact that we know what's best for them? Why do they often pay so little attention to our instructions and advice? How can they stand that music that they play over and over—especially when they insist on playing it so loud as to fracture the average eardrum? Why do they enjoy movies and TV programs that have no real plot and little redeeming social value?

Listen to the words of a great philosopher and scholar:

From the day your baby is born you must teach him to do things. Children today love luxury too much. They have detestable manners, flout authority, have no respect for their elders. They no longer rise when their parents and teachers enter the room. What kind of awful creatures will they be when they grow up?

As we worry about our young people it may give us some comfort to realize that it is not a new phenomenon. The scholar who wrote these words was Socrates, shortly before his death in 399 B.C.

The Communication Gap

The so-called "generation gap" is primarily a gap of communication. Many parents find it hard to really talk to their children, particularly during the teenage years; and, conversely, children often find it difficult to really get through to their parents. Why is this so? Though any attempt to fully explain this phenomenon would probably be an oversimplification, some of the reasons are clear.

As our society is shifting more and more to an urban way of life, Father is away a good share of the young child's waking hours—especially if he is a commuter. And, with more and more women entering the work force each year, there is more than a 50 percent chance that Mother is away a substantial part of the time too. The phenomenon of the "latchkey child" is relatively new to our society. By the way, I should point out that a mother's working outside of the home is not necessarily destructive or even detrimental to a child's self-esteem. In his book *Antecedents of Self-Esteem*, Stanley Coppersmith presents research studies which show that on the average, children of working mothers have higher self-esteem than children of nonworking mothers. Knowledge of this fact should allay some guilt feelings of mothers who work outside of the home, whether it be from financial necessity or from a need for self-fulfillment. A probable reason for higher self-esteem in children of working mothers is that they are left on their own more and do not have the parent as readily available to lean on, and as they of necessity act for themselves they develop feelings of independence and capability, and these feelings enhance self-esteem.

It is not only parents who are busy and out of the home a lot; children themselves seem to be much busier and have more activities outside the home than children in any previous generation. In far too many families home is a place to eat and sleep, and adults and teenagers are going and coming on such different schedules that it is a real challenge for parents to find the time to really communicate with their children. The dominance of television in American homes has also contributed its share to the demise of conversation among family members. For these reasons, we parents cannot rely on the routines of living to provide the communication we need with our children—we must make time to spend with our children, and strive to communicate with them.

Some of the gap in communication between parents and children is unavoidable. Children can hardly be expected to see the world through the same eyes as mature adults. And, truthfully, we are not always right. As we grow up we lose some of the freshness, the creativity, the uniqueness that we had as children. Too often we let the worries and cares of the world interfere with the natural enjoyment of life.

When a child is young there is no difficulty in understanding how he feels or what he is thinking about because he expresses it openly. This naiveté, this lack of ability or desire to deceive, is one of the refreshing qualities of young children. All too soon they learn by both precept and example that it is not always wise to express what they really think. As our children get older we may wish that we could understand them like we did when they were small. No longer do they allow us fully into their world. They share their secrets, and want to spend their time with peers, not with us. We shouldn't feel threatened when this time comes because it is normal and natural for it to happen. During the early and middle teens one of the most important tasks for adolescents is to develop a sense of autonomy and freedom from adult control. And this is good for their growing sense of self-esteem.

To be accepted and well thought of by friends is important at any age, but especially during the teen years. Young people may suddenly begin to deviate from standards of behavior that they have been taught all their lives in order to receive that acceptance. During this stage many parents find it difficult to talk to their children. But, fortunately, if the relationship has previously been good, with good communication, this situation is likely to be temporary. As children get into middle and late adolescence there is often a return to more free communication with parents again.

The Importance of Family Communication

Rhea Zakich, in a *Reader's Digest* article, tells how she learned some important secrets of family communication. She developed nodules on her vocal cords and her doctor advised her not to speak at all for at least ten days. "Impossible," she thought. "The family can't make it through the day without my coaxing and supervision." For several days she carried a notebook in her pocket to jot down instructions and answers to her family's questions. But it was a tedious process and didn't work too well. Later she had an operation on her throat to remove the nodules, and was not able to speak for several more months. She developed an awful fear that she might never speak again.

She felt herself growing away from her family, and felt a desperate need to communicate with them. She thought of how the family members had talked to one another a lot, but seldom really communicated. She decided that even if she never spoke another word, she would find a way to communicate with her family. For days she sat and thought of all the questions she wanted to ask her husband and two sons, and began to write them down on small cards. Some were serious questions like, "What is your definition of love?" Others were lighthearted like, "What do you like to do in your spare time?" Before long she had more than 200 question cards stacked on the table. Then the idea came to her to invent a board game in which the players would draw a card and answer it. This was the beginning of the "Ungame," so named because there is really no ending point on the board and no one wins and no one loses. As she played this game with her family, with them answering aloud and her writing out her answers, she learned things about her husband and sons that she never knew, and possibly would have never known, and developed increased respect for them all. Later, when the doctor pronounced her cured and she could talk again, she knew that she would never revert back to her old habits because she had learned five secrets of real communication, which she lists as follows: 1. Listen—just listen. 2. Don't criticize or judge. 3. Talk from the heart. 4. Don't assume that you know the other's thoughts and feelings. 5. Show your love.

Today, Rhea Zakich conducts communication workshops for families throughout the country. Her Ungame has sold more than one million copies in English, Spanish, French, German, and Italian and is used by counselors, teachers and psychologists throughout the world. You may wish to try this game with your own family if you have not already done so.

Fortunately, we do not have to lose our ability to speak in

order to appreciate the lessons that Mrs. Zakich learned. All of us, if we are willing to work at it, can learn to apply principles of effective communication in our homes.

Effective Family Communication Enhances Self-Esteem

The most effective key to successful communication with children is to let them know that you care. This message must come through to them clearly and unmistakably. When a child knows that parents really care, and that what he says and does is important to them, there is a big boost to self-esteem.

The knowledge that parents love and care about him can provide powerful incentives for a child to do those things that will bring about continued love and support. With this basic foundation, temporary disagreements and parental discipline that is not the very best can be overcome with no loss of self-esteem.

Improving the Quality of Family Communication

Developing effective two-way communication in a family is not always easy. But if we persist the rewards are great. Sometimes the difficulty in communication stems from the child's problems, sometimes from the adults' lack of skill, and often from a combination of both. Here are some suggestions that may help:

1. Listen more than you talk. The average parent or untrained counselor interacting with a child probably talks about 90 percent of the time and the child 10 percent. It would be well to reverse these percentages and let children

fully express themselves. There is an old homily in verse, the author of which I do not know, that goes like this:

> A wise old owl sat in an oak.
> The more he listened the less he spoke.
> The less he spoke the more he heard.
> Why can't we be like that old bird?

To most of us the sound of our own voice is the sweetest sound in the world. Yet we must realize that it is the same for others as well. Too often we are so concerned about how to insert our golden ideas into the conversation, and just how to frame them in words, that we fail to listen closely to what others are saying. We need to be careful not to let this happen with our children because we can learn about how they think and reason and view the world if we will just listen.

Rhea Zakich tells of an incident involving her nine-year-old son. One day during the time she was unable to speak he came home from school shouting, "I hate my teacher! I'm never going back to that school again." Before her vocal cord problems she might have responded with a comment such as: "Of course you are if I have to drag you there myself." But since she could not talk, she just listened. In a few minutes her angry son put his head in her lap and said, "Oh, Mom, I had to give a report and I mispronounced a word. The teacher corrected me and all the kids laughed. I was so embarrassed." The mother gave him a hug, and he was quiet for a minute. Then he jumped up, said "Thanks, Mom," and ran out to play. The mother's silence was exactly what the boy needed—just someone to confide in. He didn't need either her advice or her criticism. Mrs. Zakich remained silent from necessity. But all parents would profit at times from simply remaining silent and listening.

Most of what we tell our children in a lecturing fashion is

not new to them. They often know exactly what we are going· to say, and could finish our sentences for us if required. What our children need is less admonishing and moralizing and more listening and understanding. We need to listen to what our children are saying and try to understand the feelings that are being expressed. We don't need to always agree with a child's point of view, but we should communicate the assurance that we understand how he feels and that he has a right to these emotions. Try to remember back to what it was like to be a child in an adult-dominated world and respond to the child accordingly. When we listen, our children feel understood and worthwhile.

But, a parent says, "my child will never talk to me. I ask him how school went today, and he just grunts or gives me a very superficial answer." There could be a number of reasons for the child's reticence, and the age of the child is important. If he is in the early grades it's likely that he simply doesn't remember the events of the day very well. He lacks the ability to sequence the events of the day as an older child or adult might do. Further, he may lack the verbal skills to relate the experience very well.

When an older child and a parent have difficulty in communicating it may be because of the child's need for privacy in a world different from adults. Or it may result from a feeling that parents wouldn't really understand, perhaps because of unsuccessful attempts in the past. If we really listen to children when they are young we are more likely to be able to communicate with them as adolescents.

2. Listen actively, not passively. Carl Rogers, the father of "non-directive" or "client-centered" counseling, developed a technique known as "reflective listening," sometimes called "active listening." Other counselors have adopted this highly useful approach, and parents can use it too. In reflective listening we return the child's feelings with a comment that lets him know we understand. But it is

important to reflect back the feelings and attitudes being expressed, not merely parrot the child's own words back to him.

Here is an example of the way reflective listening might be used in a home situation.

Franz: (Age 14): How come I'm *always* the one that has to take out the garbage? Peter never has to do anything!

Dad: You feel like we give you too much to do.

Franz: Yeah! And how about Jason. His mom and dad don't make him do anything around his house.

Dad: So it isn't just your brothers. It seems like your friends don't do as much as you either.

Franz: That's for sure. His mom and dad do everything for him. He doesn't even mow the lawn. And his dad even takes the empty garbage cans around the back again.

Dad: That sounds pretty neat to have his parents do everything for him.

Franz: I guess. But his folks are nuts to do it. And he's so helpless he doesn't know how to do anything. (Exit Franz, and Dad watches him take the garbage cans out and set them on the curb.)

By the use of active listening Dad is able to understand his son's point of view. He may say to himself, "Hey, maybe we *do* expect too much of Franz and not enough of Peter. I'll have to watch that." And Franz responds to the fact that his father listens and understands him. Once he gets his feelings out he goes ahead and does the task with no further complaint. Father and son are communicating and understanding each other better, and Franz's feelings of self-worth are maintained.

Let's look at some less promising approaches that Dad might have used in answer to Franz's complaint that he was always the one to take out the garbage. (Some of these are discussed by Thomas Gordon in his well-known Parent Effectiveness Training (PET) program.)

"Now you know very well that the other kids do just as much around here as you do." (Lecturing)

"After all, son, you *are* the oldest. You can hardly expect your little brothers to be able to do as much as you." (Giving a logical argument)

"I don't want to hear another word about it. Just get out there and get the job done." (Ordering; commanding)

"One more crack like that and I'll ground you for a week!" (Warning; threatening)

"I'm really surprised at you, Franz. You're not setting a very good example." (Moralizing; preaching)

"Grow up! You're acting like a six-year-old—not a fourteen-year-old." (Shaming; ridiculing)

"You'll understand when you get older. I guess I shouldn't expect you to see the situation like a grown-up would." (Consoling; sympathizing)

"How long have you felt this way? How many kids have you talked to about what they have to do at home?" (Probing; interrogating)

"Well, just forget it for now. We'll talk about it later." (Withdrawing)

"Yes, but look at what big muscles you're getting." (Attempt at humor)

None of the above methods of responding holds much promise; and each one of them, in one way or another, is damaging to self-esteem. Even worse responses than these (physical punishment, for instance) might be mentioned. But think how surely any one of these responses will close the lines of communication between parent and child.

3. Listen to your child with both ears! Does this ever happen in your home? You are reading the paper or watching something interesting on television when one of your children comes to you with a question or with a bit of information that won't wait. You feel a need to respond to the child, yet wish the request had come at a better time. *There is no*

better time! One value of being a parent is that it makes us less selfish. We often have to turn aside from something of interest in order to talk with a child. We should set the paper down; we can't communicate effectively one-to-one and give partial attention to something else.

I know a man who is basically a good father, but he has one characteristic that interferes with communication with his children. He is an introspective person with many things running through his mind. When one of his children makes a comment or asks a question this man sometimes simply does not hear. Sometimes they will raise their voices or pull on his sleeve to get his attention. But other times, if the mother is available, it is just easier to go to her because Mom always listens. The children will make comments to her such as, "Oh, Dad's too busy," or "I *did* ask him, but he didn't hear me." Because of failure to listen, Dad misses out on opportunities for communication with his children.

We need to ask ourselves, "Do I really give my children my undivided attention, or do I sometimes try to listen while I do other things?" As we listen "with both ears," we can get to know our children better and help them to feel more important.

4. Don't be too critical. It is important for us to show respect for our children's ideas. We shouldn't expect them to be on an adult level in their thinking and reasoning abilities. We need to refrain from ridiculing or making light of their ideas or being too critical of their comments. Otherwise we can be sure that they will stop sharing their ideas with us, and we will lose the opportunity to talk with them and understand them better. Not only that, they may say to themselves, "I don't know very much," or "I'm not too bright."

We must avoid comments such as, "You should know better than that!" "We've been over that already a hundred times." "Don't be silly" "I thought you were old enough to understand." Such comments close the lines of communication and are demeaning to the child and destructive of feelings of self-esteem.

Let your child know that their ideas are important and interesting to you. In conversations with them use comments such as, "Hey, I really like that idea!" "That's an interesting point of view." "I agree with you." "That's good thinking." "Why didn't I think of that?" But a note of caution: Don't say it if you don't mean it! Children are adept at detecting insincerity, and they will resent attempts to manipulate them through flattery. Look for opportunities to boost self-esteem through sincere expressions that value your children's thought processes and intellectual capabilities.

5. Use "I messages" when appropriate. Thomas Gordon maintains that parents would do well to change most of their "you messages" to "I messages." A "you message" points an accusing finger at the child and can promote feelings of resistance and rebellion. Consider these examples: "You are a noisy pest." "You make me so mad!" "You never take the garbage out without being reminded a dozen times." "You're acting like a baby!"

Less resistance and better feelings would be maintained by changing these "you messages" to "I messages." "I can't handle all this noise. It makes me nervous and cranky." "I feel my stomach starting to churn; I don't like feeling angry." "I hate to mention the garbage again; I'm beginning to feel like a nag." "I don't think I should make your bed; I've already got more work of my own than I can do." "I messages" don't solve all problems of communication by any means, but they do get the parent's message across in a way that is less likely to put the child on the defensive and generate angry feelings.

6. Make sure that much of your communication with your children is positive and fun. If the only time we talk with our children is when we have something for them to do or

want to correct their behavior, conversations with Mom or Dad are not likely to be welcomed. Amusing anecdotes, stories, jokes, and meaningful questions can all add sparkle to conversations with our children. It will also help if we talk about things that are of interest to them. Dale Carnegie says that if you want someone to like you, talk about what he is interested in. He recalled a dinner in which he got the person next to him talking about his main field of interest. Carnegie listened and nodded his head, but said very little. He was amused when leaving the party to hear this man tell the host that he was glad to have had the opportunity to sit next to a "brilliant conversationalist!" We can apply this principle of speaking about the other person's interests to conversations with our own children. They will enjoy talking to us, seek opportunities to be with us and develop feelings that will contribute to self-esteem.

CHAPTER 13

Teach Your Child to Value Others

Serve and thou shalt be served. If you love and serve men, you cannot, by any hiding or stratagem, escape the remuneration.

—Emerson

Ron is a fourteen-year-old boy who never seems to have anything good to say about anyone. Words in his vocabulary that are much overworked are "stupid," "weird," "loser," "idiot," and "mental retard." He is ready to fight at the least provocation. Woe to the person who is shoved into him while standing in the school lunch line! Inadvertent actions and idle comments are often taken personally and interpreted negatively. Ron is a loner; because of his attitudes, children ignore him "like the plague."

How does Ron feel about himself? As you might expect, his treatment of others is merely a reflection of his own poor self-concept; he covers it up with bluster. His hostile speech and poor behavior invite criticism and rejection, which in turn further deflates his already low self-esteem.

Ron has adopted an interesting defense mechanism called "projection" in order to try to protect his ego. This is a process wherein one sees his own undesirable traits in others. Have you noticed that it is often the dishonest person who is most quick to accuse others of dishonesty? The selfish person who complains about selfishness in others? The unkind person who perceives those around him as unkind? The person who projects his faults to others is trying to hide these traits even from himself.

The Self-Others Connection

An article by Herbert Sprigle called "The Self-Others Concept" appears in *The Self-Concept of the Young Child*, a book edited by Thomas D. Yawkey. Sprigle suggests that it is important to consider not only the child's self-image, but also what he names the *self-others concept*. This is the view the child has of adults and of peers as a result of real-life experiences he has with them. The others concept considers the thoughts and feelings of other people, and sensitivity to their actions. It also includes a belief that others matter.

There is an interrelationship between feelings about one-self and feelings about others. Too often we teach children that false modesty is a virtue. They need to know that there is nothing wrong with liking oneself and feeling good about personal qualities. Positive attitudes toward others and positive attitudes toward self are interrelated and support each other.

The infant and toddler are totally self-centered by nature. They do not have the capacity to understand, let alone care about, the welfare and feelings of others. But as a child grows older he should learn by parents' words and example to be able to set aside his own needs and feelings and be considerate about the needs of others. Sprigle says that although parents have to some degree their own well-being in mind, consciously or unconsciously, when they teach the child to be concerned about others, they really have the child's well-being at heart even more. They understand intuitively the importance of the self-others connection. Wise parents know that a developing child needs to feel competent, wanted, and loved, and needs other people. Through building healthy relationships with others he values them and himself to a greater degree. To believe the parent or teacher can build up the child's self-importance without balancing it with the importance of others is to ignore the child's basic nature. Self-importance goes hand in hand with a recognition of the importance of others. It isn't really possible to truly value oneself without valuing others.

We spoke in an earlier chapter about Donald Felker's idea that a good way to teach positive self-concepts is to teach children to praise themselves, and that a good way to do this is for adults to model the behavior for the child by praising themselves. This is a difficult concept for many people; it seems immodest. Continual "blowing of one's own horn" is irritating and counterproductive. Nonetheless, parents who feel good about themselves and their accomplishments are much better models for children than those who are self-deprecating.

Family members who value one another have a mutual positive effect upon self-esteem. Family traditions and family pride provide strong support for a child in acquiring and maintaining feelings of self-worth. "We Silvers are honest, or good readers, or socially successful. Since I am a Silver, I possess these virtues, and am a good person." Fortunate is the child who is raised in a family where family members hold one another in high esteem.

Self-Centeredness and Self-Esteem

It's good for a person to like himself. But doesn't feeling good about oneself cause one to become self-centered? Think for a moment about a person you know who seems to have high self-esteem. Is this person self-conscious, easily embarrassed, overly concerned about appearances? Does he continuously talk about himself; try to make himself appear better than others? Is he unconcerned about others' feelings; unwilling to listen to another's views? Does he seem vain and conceited? The almost certain answer to each of these questions is "no." The apparent self-esteem of a person who is always talking about himself and disparaging others is sham. The person with true self-esteem does not have to constantly think about himself and is more apt to be concerned about others than is one with low self-esteem. Good feelings about self and good feelings about others are not incompatible, they are mutually supportive.

Teach Your Children to Value Other People

As parents we can help our children to see the good in others. Let's examine a few ways that are effective:

1. Be a good model for your child. It's very difficult for parents to teach a child any behavior that they do not exemplify. If we are continually finding fault, emphasizing human weaknesses, and "nit-picking," our children will probably learn to do the same. A poem written by an unknown author goes like this:

> There is so much good in the worst of us,
> And so much bad in the best of us,
> That it ill behooves any of us
> To find fault with the rest of us.

We need to minimize scandalous conversation in our homes, and set a good example of valuing other people. Look for good things about people that you can point out and talk about with your children.

There is a woman in our neighborhood who stands out as a fine example of looking for the good in others. We have known her well for more than twenty years, and never in all that time have we heard her say anything of a derogatory nature about anyone. If she is in a group of people where a juicy bit of gossip or a mean comment about someone comes up, she never joins in the salacious or petty discussion. Instead, what she will often do is mention some redeeming quality of that person, or a good deed they have done. She is able to change the tone of the conversation in such a subtle and tactful way that others in the group are scarcely aware of what has occasioned the shift. This woman's children seem to have benefited from her example and are on their way to becoming the same kind of people.

2. Emphasize the positive, and minimize the negative. There seems to be a human tendency to dwell on the bad things that people do. Our daily papers are filled with accounts of human error, folly, and conflict. Only occasionally is there a story which tells of courage, kindness, and integrity. It's sad that it is the negative that makes headlines and is featured in television news. Yet we can take comfort in the fact that one reason that positive events seldom make headlines is that goodness is commonplace. Most people are basically good, and their desirable characteristics outweigh their undesirable ones. We need to look for these good traits in people. In our interactions with our children we should help them to look for examples that present human nature at its best.

Help your children to be optimistic about the world. There is an old story told of two brothers—one a gloomy pessimist, the other a cheerful optimist. One Christmas the parents decided that they would see if they could reduce some of the differences in their two sons. So they bought for the pessimist son a roomful of the latest, most attractive toys; and for the optimistic son they stacked the barn full of manure. On Christmas morning the first son looked at the toys, complained that what he really wanted was not there, and then played with the toys for a short time before declaring he was "bored." The parents looked around for the second son and found him out in the barn cheerfully and enthusiastically digging through the manure. They asked him why he was not disappointed—why he was so cheerful. His answer was, "With all this manure there's sure to be a pony here somewhere!"

The story, of course, is mythical. But we do find, sometimes in the same family, children who are this different in their outlooks on life. While we certainly would not give an optimistic child "manure," we would certainly hope to find some ways to help a pessimistic child to see the beauties of life. We would not accomplish this by indulging him with material possessions. Like the child in the story, some children can never get enough "things" to make them happy. Trying to talk him out of his pessimistic attitude is unlikely to be effective either. Perhaps the best technique in handling such a child would be to set a happy tone ourselves and try to pay special attention to the child when he is being optimistic. Giving a child attention for pessimistic behavior is a sure way to encourage it to continue.

3. Be selective in the books, movies and television programs your children watch. Eleanor Johnson has three children, ages 11, 9, and 5. She has a part-time job which takes her away from home several evenings a week. Her husband, Charles, works at an industrial plant which requires a change of shift every few weeks. On the evenings the parents both work, the children are left alone from the time they get home from school until their mother arrives at

about 10:00 P.M. Often she finds them "glued" to the television set, where they have been for most of the evening. Recently Eleanor told her friend how grateful she is for television. "I know the kids are almost always home at night, and not out running the streets." Mrs. Johnson sees her TV set as an inexpensive baby sitter; but she has no control over the quality of the programs her children are watching.

Probably never before in the history of the world have children been exposed to such a variety of ideas and philosophies. While much of this material may support your value system quite well, some of it is probably at variance with what you want your children to learn. Many things on television are not only superficial, trivial, and time-wasting, but potentially corrupting as well. Sometimes, in an attempt at humor, deceit and subterfuge are promoted, while virtue and integrity are made to look foolish. Parents who leave their children unattended do them a real injustice. It is important for parents to know what programs their children are watching, what movies they are attending, and what reading materials are cluttering up their minds. We need to help our children to select programs and stories that reflect human nature at its best.

Public television has some wonderful programs. The nature and science programs, for example, are fascinating. "Sesame Street" is not only very appealing to young children, but highly educational as well. We should encourage our children to give the public channels a try, and help them to make the programs on these channels a significant part of their television diet.

At the same time we extoll the virtue of exposing our children to "good" movie and television watching, we need to realize that horror movies such as *Halloween* and *Friday the 13th* are not really that terrible for most children. They are part of growing up. They are so obviously outrageous and out of the realm of normal human experience that children watching them take them for what they are—sheer fantasy. Subtle movies that are less frightening, but closer to real life, are actually more difficult for children to deal with. Exposing ourselves to scary rides at the carnival and horrifying movies adds to the excitement of life, and only very seldom do they exert any harm. An exception, obviously, would have to be made for young children who are still struggling to separate out fantasy from real life.

4. Promote an understanding and acceptance of people of different racial, religious, and ethnic groups. Just as it is desirable to help our children see the good in individuals, it is also necessary to help them to develop good attitudes toward minority groups and people of other cultures. Prejudices and intolerance often develop most strongly in persons who are insecure and who have personal feelings of inferiority. It is all too easy to go along with the cultural stereotypes that label racial or ethnic groups in cruel ways. We need to be careful not to perpetuate these fallacies in the minds of our children. Invite people of minority groups to your home, and encourage your children's friendships with people of all racial, ethnic, and religious groups. We should be accepting of people of other cultures primarily because it is the fair and ethical thing to do. Racial prejudice is simply wrong. Our children are likely to identify with our values and learn to be tolerant as well. And favorable attitudes they develop toward people in general will transfer to good feelings toward themselves, enhancing self-esteem.

5. Discourage tattling and gossip. Children love to get attention from parents and teachers by reporting on the bad things other children are doing. One thing that makes this problem difficult to handle is that we are often grateful for the information that the tattler brings. Nonetheless it is obvious that tattling needs to be discouraged. One approach that can be used is to help children get the same kind of

attention in a more desirable way by reporting on the good things they see other children doing.

There is an elementary school located in the lower income area of a city. Let's call it the Thomas Jefferson School, though this is not its real name. Many of the parents are unemployed and on welfare; others are in unprestigious, low-paying jobs. There are many single parent families. In a neighborhood such as this, one might expect to find indifferent attitudes toward education and poor community support for the school. But this is not so. The principal and school psychologist have worked very hard to promote parental involvement, and teachers are encouraged to look for every opportunity to send home good news about the children in their classes. A phone call or note often informs parents of something good that their child has done. Every week there is a "Jefferson Good Guy" award given. Any child or teacher in the school can nominate a student to receive this award; but, of course, no one can nominate himself. The award includes a certificate and a pen that has "Jefferson Good Guy" printed on it. The child who nominates the winner for the week gets the recognition of having his own picture prominently displayed in the hall along with the child he nominated. Children at this school get in the habit of looking for good things they can report about each other. A special emotional climate has emerged, and the children have an increased chance of developing good levels of self-esteem. And greater self-esteem will lead to a chance for a better life.

Teach your Children to Help Other People

Along with helping our children to look for the good in others, we should teach them the joy of service. An old adage says, "We love whom we serve." As we teach our children to find pleasure in helping others, a very real by-product is growth in their own feelings of self-worth.

Herbert Sprigle, mentioned earlier in this chapter, discusses the relation of serving others to self-esteem by saying that self-importance without others-importance is self-delusion. He further states that in real life one who does not feed is not fed (at least for long).

There are many effective ways of teaching children to learn to help others. Let's examine a few of them:

1. Set a good personal example of service. Do your children often see you helping other people? Most of us could probably improve in this area. When neighbors are in the hospital, do you visit them? How long has it been since you went to visit that elderly man or woman in your neighborhood who is confined to a wheelchair? After a snowstorm do you hurry to shovel the walk of the elderly widow a few houses away? When people are experiencing car trouble are you willing to take the time to render assistance? Your child is much more likely to learn to serve others if you model that role for him.

Do you participate in worthwhile community service projects? Are there agencies in your city that are in need of volunteers? Is there a rest home, mental hospital, or prison that would open its doors to visits from you and your family? Look for an opportunity to get yourself or perhaps the whole family involved. You can also make your own family projects by visiting lonely or handicapped people, helping a senior citizen with household repairs or yard work, or other worthwhile projects.

2. Emphasize the joy of giving rather than receiving. Make holidays and birthdays times when your children experience the joy of giving and of serving others. Give them an opportunity to earn money that they can use to buy gifts for family members and friends. When possible, help your children to make gifts for each other instead of buying

them; this will enable them to put more of themselves into the gift-giving and make the gifts more special, as well as making it easier on the family budget.

Patty Carter came running into the house one day to talk to her mother. She had just learned from her friend Dolores Perez that her family was not going to celebrate Christmas that year. Dolores' father had recently lost his job, and the roof of the home had caved in and needed to be replaced. There simply wasn't going to be money for Christmas presents—or even a Christmas tree. That night Patty's family had a meeting to decide how they could help this other family. It happened that the Carters had the same number of children as the Perez family, and approximately the same ages. The suggestion was made that each child on Christmas morning pick one of his presents and give it to a member of the other family. Though the idea was hard for the youngest children in the family to accept, and even harder to actually do when the time came, all finally agreed. The Carters' custom was to have two Christmas trees—one upstairs and one down, but they decided to leave the second tree on the Perez porch a week or so prior to Christmas. Now, years later, when the subject of their favorite Christmas comes up, this is the Christmas that they most remember. The concern for others which the Carter family have displayed through the years has made them a respected family in their neighborhood. And this respect has had a reciprocal effect on the self-esteem of family members.

3. Teach your children the joy of anonymous service. Many charitable donations are made with the hope of gaining favorable publicity and earning the good will of those who are served. We should teach our children to do good for others without any expectation of a reward. Glenn Jorgenson, author of a "Positive Action Theory of Behavior"—a series of instructional tapes—suggests that it is good to give children opportunities to "practice doing

something nice without getting caught." Shining a brother or sister's shoes, making their bed, or making them a treat without letting them know who did it is a far better kind of trick than one that is nasty and causes embarrassment or inconvenience. It can be a fun game that will generate warm feelings in both the child that is served and the one who anonymously provides the service. It's just possible that if the recipient doesn't know who his benefactor is he may have to be nice to everybody in the family, and that wouldn't be a bad result. And if the person who did the nice trick is eventually discovered, some other good things can happen in the relationship of the two children who are involved.

Let's see how this might work in your family. Suppose two of your children have had a falling out and are very angry with each other. One of them tells you he feels like going into the other one's room and taking or destroying something. As you quietly talk with your child and let him ventilate his feelings, you suggest that instead of following his natural feelings of hurting his brother or sister, he secretly do something good. It may not be easy to convince the child to do something nice for his "enemy," especially while the emotional feelings are high. But if and when he does finally agree, the results are almost sure to be beneficial. You and your child can secretly enjoy the befuddlement of the other child as he tries to determine the identity of his secret pal. The very act of doing something good for the other child will lead to warmer feelings and more of a chance for enhancement of self-esteem.

As you apply these suggestions for teaching your children to value and help others, self-esteem among family members is almost sure to increase.

CHAPTER 14

Encourage Creativity in Your Child

Imagination is more important than knowledge.
            —Albert Einstein

In the story "The Little Boy," by Helen E. Buckley, the boy's teacher tells the class that they are going to make a picture. He liked to make pictures, and he begins to make all kinds of interesting things. But his teacher says that they are going to make flowers, and to wait for instructions. The little boy begins to make pink and orange and blue flowers. But once again he is stopped by the teacher, who shows them how to make a red flower with a green stem. This situation is followed by others in which the teacher always shows the children just how to do each activity. And the little boy learns to wait, and to watch, and to make things just like the teacher. And soon he doesn't make things of his own anymore. Then, on his first day at a new school, the teacher tells the class to make a picture; and the boy waits for the teacher to show him how. But she doesn't say anything and just walks around the room. When she asks the little boy why he isn't making a picture, he asks what he should make. When told he can make anything he wants and use whatever colors he wants, he begins to make a red flower with a green stem.

Creativity is a natural endowment that is present in varying degrees in all children. Almost all parents and teachers want children to be creative, yet sometimes they unwittingly stifle that creativity. The typical child enters kindergarten excited and anxious to learn. But by the third or fourth grade too many children have become "turned off" and have lost much of their native curiosity, interest, and enthusiasm.

Conformity and creativity are to a large extent incompatible, and too often we stress the former at the expense of the latter. While a certain amount of conformity is necessary to socialization, and to the peace and well-being of teachers and parents, the overconforming child is one who lacks creativity. Most school learnings involve *convergent* thinking, in which the teacher teaches the accumulated wisdom of the ages. But creativity involves *divergent* thinking, in which a person may go off on a tangent and think about something in his own unique way. This type of thinking is probably what got Edison and Einstein into trouble with their teachers, causing them to be labeled "stupid" and "unteachable." Without divergent thinking nothing new would be invented.

The creative person is one who sees things around him in fresh ways. Rigid, inflexible people cannot be creative. Only a small percentage of people in the world will produce great works of music, literature, and art. But creativity can be expressed in many regular life activities; opportunities for creative thinking and expression are everywhere. A child can learn to use his own individuality to add zest and enjoyment to his life.

The Relationship of Creativity to Self-Esteem

There is a strong relationship between creativity and self-esteem, and this relationship is reciprocal: creative accomplishment helps a child to feel good about himself, and feeling good about himself helps a child to be creative. In order to be truly creative children must believe in themselves and be willing to accept the risk of trying out new things. Most creative children have an abundance of self-confidence and initiative. A child with low self-esteem is apt to suppress creative ideas. He does not trust his own judgment, and he fears disapproval of others. Conformity is not as much fun as creativity, but it is much safer.

Creative thought and expression help children to feel good about themselves. As they demonstrate to adults, to peers, and to themselves that they have the ability to solve problems and master their environment, feelings of capability and self-esteem will blossom. Creativity is often an individual matter, and a child's imaginative ideas cannot and should not be labeled as "right" or "wrong." Creativity thrives best in an environment that is accepting and nonjudgmental.

Parents need to be concerned as much about creative expression in their children as they are about academic accomplishment. Thomas D. Yawkey, in his book *The Self-Concept of the Young Child*, has written a section called "Creative Thinking and Self-Concept in Young Children." He maintains that creative thinking and expression not only contribute to but are actually the basis of a "fourth basic R," which is just as essential to a child as the traditional "reading, 'riting, and 'rithmetic." He says, also, that creative thinking is linked with self-esteem, and suggests ways to nurture it. Cultivating creative thinking helps self-esteem to grow and develop.

Suggestions for Enhancing Creativity in Children

The type of home environment that children experience has much to do with how they think. Parents can use techniques that stimulate a child's imagination and creative abilities, or they can resort to child-rearing practices that inhibit and suppress creative expression. Here are some suggestions of ways in which you can enhance creativity in your children:

1. Use praise and positive reinforcement. Mrs. Tucker's three children have a reputation among their friends of being artistic. Recently a neighbor asked her, "Do your kids get their artistic abilities from you or from your husband?" Her reply was, "Well, as a matter of fact, neither John nor I are especially artistic. But we've encouraged our kids in art and made art materials available. We make it a point never to say anything critical about their pictures. Instead we look for something good to say. If they use the whole page instead of just drawing something in one corner, we tell them how pleased we are that they used the whole paper. If they use colors that go together well, we comment about that."

When a child brings you some of his creative work, look for something you can sincerely praise. Hang your children's pictures up on the wall. Encourage them to make up stories and illustrate them with their own drawings. Sometimes you might even want to bind them together into a book.

You will want to save some samples of creative work that your children do. It will be interesting for you and for them to look at their art work in future years.

2. Avoid ridicule. Marcia, age 5, made a crayon drawing of a woman. "What's that?" asked her eight-year-old

brother. "I'm making a picture of Mommy," she answered. Mark laughed derisively and snatched up the picture. He ran into his older sister's bedroom with Marcia in hot pursuit. "Hey, look at this weird picture Marcia made. It's supposed to be a picture of Mom." Carol and Mark had a good laugh about the drawing and then together went to show it to their mother. "Want to see what you look like, Mom?" asked Carol. Mother smiled, and then noticing that Marcia had followed her sister and brother into the room and was beginning to cry, decided that she had better come to the little girl's defense. "You two should be ashamed of yourselves making fun of Marcia. After all, she's just five, and you can't hardly expect her to draw like you do. It's pretty good for her age." The ridicule of her brother and sister, coupled with the "faint praise" of her mother, left Marcia devastated. What an effective way to stifle a child's creative impulses!

When your young child shows you a picture he has drawn it is sometimes impossible to make out what it is supposed to be. Either a guess that proves to be wrong or a question about what it is supposed to be can be discouraging to the child. A better approach is to say something like this, "How nice. Tell me about your picture."

It is a good idea to avoid criticism of any kind of artistic or creative work that a child does. A parent or teacher can stifle creative writing by attending too much to spelling or grammatical errors. When the main intent of an English paper is to stimulate and assess creativity, the teacher would do well to temporarily suspend the marking of grammatical errors, or do it on a separate sheet. The pointing out of poor features or mistakes in any artistic production can undermine a child's feelings of competency and self-esteem and promote a reluctance to try again.

3. Encourage independent actions and exploration. I know a mother who wants so much to keep her children from

danger and possible harm that she constantly monitors every activity. When other children in the neighborhood go on an outing or participate in some activity, this woman does not allow her children to be included. She always imagines the worst thing that could happen, and on the rare occasions that her children are away from her jurisdiction she suffers mental agony until they return. She discourages any exploration that has any messiness, mild danger, or inconvenience associated with it.

It is impossible to protect a child completely from every possible danger. While parents have an obligation to anticipate possible hazards and keep children from serious harm, they must be allowed to participate in activities which involve some risks. Children who are kept in an antiseptic environment and treated like hothouse plants are likely to either become unduly dependent or to break away from parental control and become incorrigible. In neither case are they likely to develop much self-esteem or creativity.

4. Listen to your child's suggestions and respect his ideas. There is a story, said to be true, of a trucker who tried to go under an overpass that was slightly too low. The truck became stuck, and all attempts of the driver and his helper to free it were futile. A small boy happened along and watched the activity with some interest. After a few minutes he approached the driver and said, "Mister, I know how you can get your truck loose." The man's answer was, "Son, you'd better run along. You might get in the way and get hurt." The boy retreated some distance, but after a while he tried again. This time the helper said, "Hey, it won't hurt to see what the kid's idea is," and in desperation the driver agreed. "Take a little air out of the tires," the boy said. And in a few minutes the truck was free and on its way again.

How willing are you to listen to your children's ideas? A

child can often see things from a different perspective than an adult, and sometimes his sight is clearer, as in the example above. Listening to your child and accepting his ideas will foster creative thinking. Comments such as, "I like that idea," or "That's good thinking" will encourage a child and contribute to feelings of confidence.

5. Have creative materials in your home. Mozart wouldn't have composed simple melodies at age three if there hadn't been a piano in his home. Likewise, your child's creative abilities have a better chance to appear if there are creative materials available to him. Paper, scissors, clay, paints, paste, ribbons, colored cloth, blocks, sand and simple musical instruments and old clothes are all helpful in stimulating imagination and creativity.

Especially valuable in encouraging creativity in children are materials that have more than one function and can be used in a variety of ways. These need not be expensive. A large cardboard box that the new refrigerator or stove came in can provide hours of amusement and creativity as it changes from a house, to an office, to a school room, to a jail, or any number of other uses. A carpet end tube can be a telescope, a cannon, or just something to look through or shout through. Young children want to have a close personal experience with objects—to be able to handle them, listen to them, and even smell and taste them.

In addition to informal materials that can be made available to children to stimulate creative activities, there are also educational games such as Password, Concentration, Picture or Word Bingo. Constructional materials such as table and floor blocks, Lincoln Logs, Tinker Toys, and Lego sets and puzzles of various kinds also foster creative abilities. Video games and audio tapes can stimulate children's imagination. If you are fortunate enough to have a home computer, the possibilities for creative activity are boundless.

6. Enter into creative play with your children. Yawkey, mentioned earlier in the chapter, says that playful adults are more likely to encourage, support, and reinforce creative thinking and a good self-concept. Parents and teachers can use both playful gestures and playful statements in dealing with young children. Examples of playful gestures would be pretending to eat or drink, pretending to be an airplane landing on a runway, pretending to be an astronaut, pretending to be a Maypole around which children can dance and sing. Examples of playful statements or questions might be, "I like the way your baby giggles!" as the child role-plays being the mother. "What would it be like to be as big as an elephant? As tiny as a bumblebee?" "If your dog could talk, what would he say to you?"

Most young children respond quite well to role-playing. Either real-life situations or fanciful ones such as fairy tales can be used. It is interesting occasionally to reverse the roles, with the child acting out the role of a parent and the adult role-playing being a child.

A note of caution might be advised here. Some people are much more comfortable in creative play with children than are others. You may wish to practice these techniques and develop more proficiency; you will become more spontaneous as you learn to relax more. But if you feel shy or uncomfortable, don't feel that you need to use them. Use the other suggestions that are more suited to your personality.

7. Participate in fun activities with your children. Helen and Ty Jensen set one evening a week aside to do things with their children. No business or social obligations are allowed to interfere with this commitment. Creative activities and games take a top priority. Sometimes the family goes on a bicycle ride or takes a nature walk, and the parents stimulate interesting discussions about things that are seen along the way. At different times they have visited a

bakery, the fire station, a copper mine, a steel manufacturing plant, a television station, and similar attractions. Various family members participate in rhythmic dancing, singing, playing musical instruments, dramatics, painting, and ceramics. These activities have broadened the children's experiences and stimulated an interest in things around them. They have also generated feelings of family closeness and solidarity and an esprit de corps that contributes to a feeling of belonging and self-esteem.

8. Help your child to become aware of the beauties around him. How long has it been since you sat with your child and watched a sunset, the snow gently falling, a waterfall, trees covered with colored leaves, or some other beauty of nature? Some of the most beautiful things in the world go largely unnoticed. Did you ever stop to think how amazing a sunset would be if it occurred only once or twice in a lifetime, like Halley's Comet does? People would travel clear around the world to see it. But because sunsets occur so often as to be commonplace, only the most spectacular ones get our attention.

Help to sensitize your child to the beautiful things in his environment. Point out some of the interesting features that he might otherwise not notice. Talk together about the way these things make you feel. Studying the stars together on a warm summer evening, with or without a telescope, can be a worthwhile experience for you and for your child. Focusing in on the splendor of our environment will create good feelings about the world around us and help creativity to blossom.

9. Stimulate your child's imagination. A young child lives in a world of imagination. You should do everything you can to stimulate and encourage such imagination because life itself tends to stifle imagination as one grows older. Children as young as three love to pretend, and you should enter actively into such activities.

Until age five or six children have difficulty in separating out what is real and what is not real. They may be disturbed by things that they see in a movie or on television because they think the events are actually happening. For this reason you should be careful about what movies or television programs they watch. Even fairy tales are not the best fare for such minds, not so much because of the violence that is in them, though this can be a factor, but because they are more enjoyable and less confusing when the child is a little older and has a clear recognition of the difference between fantasy and reality. Before age six the kind of stories and books that are most interesting and most beneficial to the child are picture books and factual representations of people and objects in his real world.

Creative play activities can help to bridge the gap between imaginary and real people and problems. Parents can ask children to predict, "What would happen if . . . ?" and then develop imaginative role-playing situations from the child's answers.

Mutual storytelling activities can be fun for children and can help to foster creativity. In this method the parent is usually the one to begin telling a story, though after trying it several times the child can be encouraged to begin one. Each participant, the parent and the child, take the story as far as they wish and then stop and turn it over to the other to continue. They alternate in this way until one or the other decides to bring the story to an end.

By age seven or eight children are able to differentiate quite well between fantasy and reality. But they enjoy pretending and may sometimes exaggerate the sights and sounds around them to "spice up" their lives or get attention from adults. For example, Connie sees a red sunset behind the neighbor's house and rushes home to tell her mother that Morgan's house is on fire. Or Joe sees a minor automobile accident and later tells his dad that six people were killed. Sometimes it is hard to know whether a child of this age really believes a story he has told that is obviously untrue. It is best for a parent not to get concerned when a young child makes up an exaggerated story, and punish him for being a "liar." Rather than stifle the imagination that is associated with these "lies," you might try a touch of humor: "Boy, Connie sure has a good imagination," or "Joe can really make up good stories!" You might even encourage the child to write down the stories, or write them for him if he is too young to write them himself, and perhaps even encourage him to draw pictures to illustrate them. They might even be bound and made into a book. By encouraging the child to use his imagination and make up stories, but letting him know that you know they are not true, you encourage creativity without letting your child manipulate you.

10. Make wise use of television. In an earlier chapter we told of Mrs. Johnson, who used television as an inexpensive baby sitter while working outside the home. The emphasis was upon the need to know what values are being promoted in our children's lives. But there are some other dangers of television that are worthy of mention. It can also be a time-waster and can keep children from activities that would be more valuable and more creative.

It may appear that television would promote creativity and imagination in a child, but this is not the case. Since the people and events are portrayed clearly and directly, as though they were real, there is little need for imagination. Radio drama, which was common before the days of television but is now almost nonexistent, was a much better medium for the stimulation of imagination. Even better was active play such as cops and robbers, cowboys and Indians, and similar games. I remember as a child how a ladder placed over a wooden box with a table leaf across it became an airplane, the rungs of the ladder being seats for the passengers. My friends and I could play for hours in this "airplane," devising all kinds of hair-raising adventures. We see little of this kind of activity today, as children opt for the much easier and less challenging activity of turning on a dial.

Television watching is especially regrettable when it is a substitute for reading. Television can be a "mindless" activity, with little or no real thought required, whereas reading in order to be meaningful must be an active process. Good reading can open up to a child a rich world of imagination. Fortunate is the child who grows up in a home where appreciation for books is taught from babyhood—where books are prized possessions and trips to the library are frequent.

11. Encourage free play, and don't structure your child's life too much. Kendall's father feels that it is important for a child to learn to work if he is going to get ahead in the world. The chores that he has assigned the boy take almost two hours an evening to accomplish. He has also arranged for Kendall to have a paper route, and the boy has to get up at 6:00 A.M. in order to get the papers delivered before he goes to school. Kendall's mother is anxious to provide her children with cultural opportunities which she lacked as a child. Besides piano and trumpet lessons, she has arranged for Kendall to be enrolled in a drama club that meets on Saturday mornings. Kendall's parents both have worthy motives. They love him and are acting in ways that they think are in his best interest. But between the two of them they have managed to structure this ten-year-old's life to the point that he has very little time for himself. Children in the neighborhood seldom come over after school or on Saturdays because they have learned that Kendall never has time to play.

Play is an important ingredient in a child's life. While it is crucial for children to learn to work and accept responsibility, it is imperative that parents not overdo a good thing. A child should not have his life structured to the point that he doesn't have time to just be a kid. Every child should have a chance to put his feet in the brook, lie on his back and watch the clouds drift by, build castles in the sand and in the air, and engage in many other unstructured activities if he is to be free to develop imagination and creativity.

12. Help your child to accept failure realistically. Angela, a nine-year-old girl, is described by her teacher as a child who is "very difficult to motivate." Often after an assignment is given she will just sit and look into space rather than begin the task. Her teacher doesn't know what to make of this behavior, but assumes it to be an act of defiance. He reacts to it by increasing the pressure upon Angela to get to work. What Angela's teacher does not know is that her inactivity is not directed toward him at all, but it is a reaction to her own feelings of ineptness and low self-esteem. She is convinced that she will not be able to do well and does not want to expose herself to possible ridicule. She would rather be thought of as uncooperative than inept.

Help your child to realize that everyone fails at times. He will be far less threatened by his own failures if he sees you acknowledging your own mistakes and facing up to them realistically, rather than trying to cover them up. Admit your errors openly with comments such as, "Well, I really botched that up!" or "It looks like I was wrong about that." If your children see that even Mom and Dad make mistakes and fail at times they will develop less fear of failure themselves. Children need to be able to expose themselves to possible failure if they are to have the self-confidence and initiative that they need to be creative.

13. Say "no" to your child only when it is necessary. Controlling a child too much can be just as undesirable as controlling him too little. Saying "no" too often can either inhibit your child and make him dependent and afraid to try

things on his own, or have the opposite effect and make him rebellious and determined to have his own way in spite of your wishes.

Before we say "no" we should ask ourselves, "What difference will it make?" We may find that in many cases there is no justifiable reason for forbidding the child to do the thing that is in question. Children need to be free of unnecessary restrictions if they are to develop the initiative for creative endeavor.

CHAPTER 15

Help Your Child Maintain Good Health and Personal Appearance

> **Look to your health; and if you have it, praise God, and value it next to a good conscience; for health is the second blessing that we mortals are capable of; a blessing that money cannot buy.**
>
> —*Izaak Walton*

Good health and good physical appearance are related to each other, though it is possible to have one without the other. Both are closely related to self-esteem.

Bart was a sixth-grade boy whom I met once a week with four other boys in a counseling group. He sometimes had a noticeable body odor, and one day one of the other boys in the group said, "Bart, you stink!" Though Bart did not respond, I could tell he was hurt by the remark. Bart was a shy, sensitive boy, and this rude comment was one more blow to his self-esteem.

Sandra was an eighth-grade girl who was noticeably overweight. She seemed to take the good-natured kidding of her friends in stride, and in fact she was often the one who initiated it or told a joke on herself. Her technique was to "beat them to the punch." Outwardly she was not bothered by her size, but inwardly she was hurting. She maintained a jolly exterior to cover up her pain and to be accepted by others.

Jay could be found lying on a cot in the health clinic at his school quite frequently. Almost daily he complained to his third-grade teacher that his stomach hurt or that he had a headache. In any kind of competitive activity in the classroom or on the playground Jay excused himself from participation by saying that he did not feel well.

What did Bart, Sandra, and Jay all have in common? One quality they shared was low feelings of self-worth. It's difficult for a child to generate self-esteem when he doesn't look good, or doesn't feel well. Later in the chapter I'll discuss the approaches we use to remove or lighten these children's problems and help their self-esteem.

The Parents' Role in Fostering Good Appearance and Good Health in Children

Children are not equally healthy or equally attractive, but parents can play a key role in enhancing the appearance and well-being of their children and getting the most out of the assets that they have. Key school personnel can also be helpful at times. Let's look at some common problems and some possible solutions to them.

1. Poor personal hygiene. Problems involving lack of personal care and cleanliness are sometimes the fault of parents who have failed to provide proper training in the home. Problems may also result from lack of motivation or perhaps even rebellion against parents or the establishment. In the case of Bart, since I had already developed a good

relationship with him, I decided on a direct approach to the problem of body odor. Since the situation had come out openly in the group session, I arranged to talk to Bart alone about it. He was hurt by the unkind remark made in the group, but didn't seem to know what he could do differently. He told me that he bathed and changed his underwear almost every day. I got him to agree to bathe and change every day. I also introduced him to deodorant by giving him a sample to try. In a very short time the body odor disappeared and Bart became better accepted by his classmates. And the positive effects on his self-esteem were amazing.

2. Obesity. In addition to the numerous health problems that can be created or intensified by obesity, the child who is noticeably overweight is very likely to have problems with his self-image, especially in our modern society which seems often to equate thinness with attractiveness.

Recent research seems to indicate that obesity is not necessarily a result of gluttony or lack of self-discipline. As a matter of fact, some people who are too heavy eat less than the average person eats. Though exercise can help, especially when combined with eating in moderation, it is no guarantee of slimness. The fact that obesity tends to run in families has been usually assumed to mean that family customs and life style are responsible. However, it has been found that adopted children compare in body type more closely to their natural parents than to their adoptive parents— more closely to natural siblings than to those they live with, indicating that heredity plays an important role. What this all means is that some children will have a much more difficult time controlling their weight than other children do. Nonetheless, there are a number of things that parents can do to help children keep their weight within reasonable limits. Here are a few:

a. Avoid scolding and ridicule. Also avoid talking continually about the child's weight problem. He already knows he is "fat," and does not need to be told again. Encouragement, and positive reinforcement for refraining from high-calorie foods, will be much more effective than any type of punishment or scolding attention.

b. Provide emotional support. People often overeat when they are under emotional pressure. Have you ever found yourself eating when you were not really hungry? This is most likely to happen at a time when you are worried or feeling emotional tension. For some children eating can be a substitute for feelings of love and acceptance. A vicious cycle can be set up: the child feels unloved, tries to compensate by taking in food, gets more and more overweight, becomes less attractive to himself and to others, and self-esteem suffers. Expressions of love and acceptance can help the cycle to move in a healthy direction, because he begins to feel loved he has less need for extra food, loses some of the excess weight, receives encouraging comments from others, and develops constructive feelings about himself.

Randy, a nine-year-old boy, was referred to me because his teacher felt he was "nervous" and couldn't concentrate on his school work. I also noted, though it was not mentioned in the referral, that he was noticeably overweight for a child his age. Part of my evaluation of Randy was a close look at his home background. I found that he lived at home with his parents and one brother, age 6. Both parents worked an evening shift, and the two children were left at home five nights a week until almost midnight. Their mother would prepare supper for them to heat in the microwave oven, but the boys did a lot of snacking in addition to the evening meal. They also would occasionally appear at a neighbor's door at 9:00 or 10:00 at night and say that they were hungry and ask if they could have something to eat. The neighbors were sympathetic to the children and critical of the parents; I'm sure they thought that the parents were leaving them at home with nothing to eat. It really wasn't food the children were looking for, but human companionship. The parents were overestimating the ability of the children to stay at home at night alone and fend for themselves; the boys were afraid to be home alone at night, but they would not admit it, even to themselves. Fear and loneliness were expressed as hunger.

c. Pay close attention to the child's diet. Are there some tasty and nutritious low-calorie foods that could be substituted for the high-calorie foods he currently enjoys? Can fresh fruits take the place of pies, cakes, and ice cream? Can fruit and vegetable juices take the place of canned soda? In the interests of helping the overweight child, the whole family may have to modify their daily menus.

d. Provide nutritious, low-calorie snacks. Make low-calorie foods such as carrot and celery sticks available. It is said that the energy involved in chewing celery uses up more calories than there are in the celery. It will not be very exciting for a child who has been used to snacking on sweets to suddenly switch to raw vegetables and other low-calorie foods. However, if these are readily available in the refrigerator, and sweets are nowhere to be found, he may decide that they are better than nothing. Unfortunately the child may ignore the celery and carrot sticks and find sources of sweets outside the home, but the more rapport that the parents can develop with the child, and the more the feeling is communicated that the parent is acting out of love in restricting the child's diet, the more chance the child will be cooperative.

e. Provide constructive reinforcement. Parents and teachers accomplish much more change in children's behavior by using constructive methods. One excellent way for a child to receive reinforcement is to chart his progress from day to day or week to week. Gains that the child can clearly see will be highly motivating and self-perpetuating.

f. Set up family rules about food consumption. One good rule, for example, is no snacks at the movies or when watching television. It is all too easy to get so engrossed in the plot of the story that you are not consciously aware of how much you are eating. Another good rule is only one small dessert and no seconds after a meal.

I found in talking with Sandra and her mother that much of the overeating that took place in the home was connected with television viewing. A favorite activity of the family was renting video movies, and buying snack foods of high calorie content. They agreed that they would be replaced by either no snacks or low-calorie snacks. This approach, combined with a moderate exercise program and some restriction of desserts, was beneficial for the mother as well as Sandra, and self-esteem was improved.

3. Undereating. Though eating too little is less likely to be a problem than is eating too much, it can be a deterrent to both good health and personal appearance for some children. While it is easy to understand the predicament of a child who doesn't eat enough because of food deprivation, it is not as easy to understand a child who doesn't eat when nutritious food is readily available.

Food refusal in a young child can occur as a result of a power struggle between the parent and the child. The more force the parent uses to get the child to eat, the more the child rebels. Parents should be calm and matter-of-fact about the child's eating or not eating. Since young children are apt to regard any new or unfamiliar food with suspicion, they should be presented with a large variety of foods from an early age. Mild encouragement should be used to have a child try at least a small portion of each food. But forcing him or punishing him for not eating are not apt to be effective, and will damage the parent-child relationship.

Serious cases of undereating can turn into anorexia nervosa, a form of voluntary starvation. Anorexia is much more common in girls than in boys; in fact it is quite rare in the male sex. A major reason seems to be that a greater premium is placed upon beauty and attractiveness for girls than for boys. And many people, male and female, equate slenderness with beauty—the thinner a girl is, the prettier she is deemed to be. So it is not too surprising when a girl eats less than good health dictates. But when the problem becomes life-threatening, there is more involved than just a normal desire to be thin and beautiful. Anorexia can sometimes be a form of self-punishment: the child punishes herself by self-starvation as an attempt to atone for feelings of guilt and worthlessness. In some girls it represents a fear of growing up and becoming a woman. Anorexia is not a problem that parents should try to cope with themselves. Professional help is needed—both physiological and psychological.

4. Medical problems. In addition to overeating or undereating, which can stem from or lead to medical problems, there are many other conditions that can have an unfortunate impact on a child's physical health, and consequently on his self-esteem. Jay, mentioned early in the chapter, is a case in point. When he was first referred to me I assumed that it was a typical case of either malingering, in which he was pretending to be ill in order not to have to interact with the other children, or of a real psychosomatic distress brought on by emotional factors at home or at school with which he had difficulty coping. However, a referral to the family doctor revealed a hormonal deficiency which was medically correctable, and within a month or two Jay was back in the classroom and on the playground, with an obvious boost to his acceptance by other children and to his own feelings of self-worth.

Another relatively common problem occurs with sensory deficits. Children with vision and hearing problems will often resist any remedial measure that calls attention to the defect. Pam's eyes were so bad that she could not see what her teachers wrote on the board unless she stood right in front of it. When reading or writing she had to hold the page close to her eyes. She was referred to an ophthalmologist, who examined her eyes and prescribed glasses. She would wear the glasses at home, with only family members to see, but absolutely refused to take them to school or wear them when her friends were around. Later she persuaded her parents to allow her to wear contact lenses. Now her school work and her self-confidence have improved dramatically.

Lois was an attractive high-school senior, but she did not see herself as attractive because she had a quite prominent bump on her nose—a family trademark. She hated to have her picture taken, and absolutely refused to be photographed in profile. She was quite introverted, had only a few friends, and she literally hated her high-school years. At the beginning of her senior year she told her parents that she had decided to have an operation on her nose, and though they offered to pay part of the cost she said that this is something she wanted to do herself. She obtained a part-time job after school and on Saturdays, and then worked full-time during the following summer. She saved all of the money needed for the operation and had it done near the end of the summer. The transformation in Lois' personality was much more dramatic that the transformation in her physical appearance. Interestingly, no one outside of her family ever found out about the operation. Her friends and acquaintances noted that there was something different about her appearance, but assumed it was due either to a change in hairstyle or to the fact that she was happier and smiled more. That fall she went on to college, and the change in her personality and enjoyment of school was dramatic.

By relating the case of Lois I am not suggesting that all girls with bumps on their noses need to have plastic surgery. Many girls with much more severe facial problems are still able to accept themselves and to be accepted by others.

Neither am I suggesting that in such cases there is always a transformation in personality or self-esteem. But the life of this one individual was made much happier, and her self-esteem was enhanced greatly by this intervention.

It is unfortunate when crooked teeth, or some other correctable defect in a child, persists and has an adverse effect on health or on self-esteem. Orthodontic treatments or correction of a skin problem may have infinitely more worth than a new automobile or a family vacation.

5. Dress and general appearance. It is important to most children that they be allowed to dress like others in their peer groups. Styles and fads sometimes seem foolish and impractical to adults, but they may seem necessary and crucial to the child, especially during the adolescent years. The coat that was handed down from an older sibling may have to be relegated to the closet or to the Goodwill bag because "nobody would be caught dead in a coat like that" this season. Rather than take a chance on being teased your child may choose to wear no coat at all, no matter how low the temperature. While a child may have to accept the fact that family finances will not allow the purchase of the most expensive and fashionable clothing, he should have the right to dress in a way that will not bring on criticism or ridicule from his peers. But there are ways of saving a great deal of money if one shops wisely, watches for sales, and is willing to buy some used clothing. Flea markets, thrift shops, and swap meets sometimes provide an opportunity to purchase clothing that is stylish and almost new for a fraction of the cost of new clothing. And shopping for bargains can be fun.

The condition in which clothing is kept is much more important than whether it is purchased new or used. There may be a valid reason for a child's wardrobe being limited, but there is really no excuse for children coming to school in filthy and tattered clothing. A child who is neat and clean has a much greater chance of gaining favorable attention and developing self-esteem than one who is dirty and unkempt.

We have talked about ways of helping children to maintain good health and personal appearance. It's true that there are some conditions related to health and appearance for which little can be done directly—for example, the boy who is unusually small for his age; or the child with a chronic health problem or physical disability. However, we still can help to maintain a child's self-esteem by accepting him as he is, by not worrying about things that cannot be changed, and by letting him know we appreciate his attractive traits.

CHAPTER 16

Self-Esteem in the Child from a Divorced Home

He is happiest, be he king or peasant,
who finds peace in his home.

—*Goethe*

Most people think of divorce as something that only happens to other people. Almost no one enters a marriage with the expectation that the arrangement is not a permanent one. But the fact is that more than one in three marriages will end in divorce. Once a rarity in American families, divorce has now become a way of life for a substantial number of people. Few families, or extended families, are untouched by it.

The 1988 edition of *Statistical Abstract for the United States* reports that in 1986 there were 2,477,000 marriages in the United States and 1,160,000 divorces, or almost one divorce for every two marriages. The number of children involved in these divorces was 1,081,000, or an average of almost one child per divorce. In 1984, 21.5 out of every

1,000 married women age 15 and older were divorced, and this is the approximate number that are divorced each year.

The rate of divorce in the United States far exceeds that of any other country. Three out of four divorces occur in families with children. It is estimated that as many as 45 percent of all children born in 1977 are likely to live for at least several months as members of a one-parent family.

Statistics such as these are frightening, but they do not tell the complete story. How many other children live in families that are not broken by divorce but have problems between the father and mother that can be just as serious, or even more serious, than if divorce had occurred? Children who are exposed to continuous parental discord, with constant bickering, demeaning statements, criticism, threats, and perhaps even physical abuse, would often be better off living with a single parent. There is something to be said for a quick and final separation early in a marriage as it becomes clear that there are unreconcilable differences that cause severe stress in one or both of the marriage partners. It is natural, and worthy, for people not to want to give up on a marriage; it may seem to be an admission of defeat—of personal failure. Often a husband or wife persists under the false hope that the spouse will change, that things will be different. But they realize too late that their expectation was not realistic. Seldom can a person change someone else. In a marriage that should have never taken place it is fortunate when the breakup occurs before there are children in the home.

Effects of Divorce on Parents

Traditionally when a divorce occurs one parent has been granted custody and the other parent given visitation rights, though there is a growing trend for courts to award joint custody. Single custody places a burden on the custodial parent. There is often a need to go back to work, which may not be easy, especially if it is the mother and she has been out of the labor market for a number of years. And often the work that is available is low in income and prestige. Returning to work creates many pressures. Some of these may occur with the work itself, but they are compounded by other factors. Working full time and then having to come home to another full-time job may sap her energy. The fatigue may make her irritable, which may be difficult for young children to understand and which may mar the limited time which she does have to spend with them.

Whether or not the mother returns to work, the family usually has to adjust to a greatly reduced income. Children often do not understand this situation and are likely to resent their deprivation: "It wasn't like this when Dad was home."

The problems of the custodial parent are exasperated when the noncustodial parent indulges the child and grants special privileges not given by the other parent. This is a common practice, and it results from a number of possible causes. There may be guilt about the breakup and about not spending time with the child, and the missing parent may try to make up for it by giving material gifts or letting the child do things he shouldn't do. The special treatment may have less worthy motives—the indulgence may be an attempt to curry special favor or to woo the child away from the custodial parent. Or the purpose may be to punish the custodial parent, who becomes the "ogre" who enforces discipline and schedules not enforced during the visitation period.

If infidelity was involved in the breakup there are apt to be serious feelings of guilt on the part of the offender and sorrow and anger at having been betrayed on the part of the offended. Either set of feelings is apt to create situations not in the best interest of either parents or children. A person who feels guilty will often resort to rationalization and self-justification and look for someone else to blame—usually the marriage partner. A person who feels offended and betrayed will often look for ways to get even. Further, self-esteem is often sorely damaged.

Effects of Divorce on Children

Most parents would agree that the divorce experience is damaging to children in many ways. Studies indicate that children of divorce are referred for psychiatric evaluation at nearly twice the rate of the nondivorced population. It has also been shown that children of divorce have more delinquent behavior and overt aggression toward their parents than do children from intact homes.

Behavioral changes that have been reported in preschool children following a divorce include regression in toilet training, increased irritability, whining and crying, separation anxiety, and mental confusion. Many of them show an inordinate need for affection which causes them to reach out too quickly to strange adults.

Unfortunately, when a marriage fails, parental direction, support, love, and discipline tend to be weakened, and children are frequently expected to fend for themselves. There are a number of reasons for this. Parents are so caught up in their own emotional needs that they become self-centered; they fail to see just how much the children are being affected. Also their energy is so sapped by their emotional turmoil that they have little left to give their children. They may not be fully aware of the children's suffering because the child may cover up feelings in order to protect the parent. A nine-year-old boy was overheard to say to his six-year-old brother: "Don't talk about Daddy in front of Mommy, because that will only make her cry more and we'll have to cheer her up."

The Effects of Divorce upon a Child's Self-Esteem

Divorce is almost certain to impact upon the self-concept of children. It is not surprising that the frustration, turmoil, feelings of guilt or anger, financial strain, and other stresses felt by one or both parents, takes its toll on the children involved, and diminishes their feelings of self-worth. The separation is almost certain to strike at the self-esteem of at least one of the parents, and the self-esteem of a child who identifies with that parent is likely to be affected as well.

It is common for a newly divorced parent to be highly emotional and hostile at times, and a child may mistakenly think that these emotions are directed toward him. He may be sensitive to the adult's emotions but not fully aware of its meaning. He may think the parent is responding to something he has done and feel guilty. Because of the parent's own emotional reactions to the many stresses that occur, there is apt to be less interaction with the child, and less reinforcement that he is valued and accepted.

When divorce occurs the child will likely be left with only one parent to provide emotional support on a daily basis. At best the other parent becomes only a visitor—and sometimes contact with the noncustodial parent is curtailed severely or altogether. A child may fear that he is so unlovable that even his own parent left him.

Changes in routines and living patterns, and parental inconsistency that often occurs at this time, may make the child withdraw or become more demanding, aggressive, rigid, or disobedient.

Suggestions for Helping Children from Divorced Homes

It is clear that divorce can cause severe stress to both parents and children. Yet sometimes it is necessary and inevitable. There are things parents can do to minimize the deleterious effects of divorce and protect the self-esteem of children caught up in it. Here are a few:

1. Let the child know that he is not at fault. It is very common for children to blame themselves for the breakup and torture themselves wondering what they should have done to prevent it. They may think back to times when they were disobedient and connect these events with the separation. "If I hadn't made Mommy mad at me so much she wouldn't have left." "If I hadn't made Mommy sad she would have been nicer, and Daddy would have liked it better at home and would have stayed." It may be that some time when he was angry at a parent the thought may have crossed his mind, "I wish she'd die!" or "I wish he wasn't my dad." Then when the separation occurs he thinks it is punishment for his bad thoughts. What a burden of guilt a child can carry around unnecessarily!

It is important that parents make it clear that the reasons for the divorce have nothing whatever to do with the child. A simple explanation of the actual reason for the estrangement will help him to understand that it is not his fault and protect his self-esteem.

2. Explain the divorce simply and in a way that is appropriate to the child's age. The full details of parental estrangement are more than the child can or should be expected to handle, but an explanation that is on the child's level and that he can understand should be given. With a four- or five-year-old the explanation might be that Daddy will not be living with them anymore, but that they will

have a chance to see him and be with him often. As children get older they are capable of, and deserve, a more complete explanation. But this should always be stated in terms the child can comprehend. "Sometimes grownups argue and make each other unhappy. When this happens sometimes they're better off not living in the same house. But we both love you very much, and Daddy will come to see you as often as he can." It is important to give honest explanations to children. It is also important to keep the discussion limited to specific things that are really happening rather than speculating about what may or may not happen. It is best for children to understand that it is neither parent's fault—that they have simply decided that they would be happier not living together anymore. Statements should be avoided that place blame on either parent: "Daddy has done bad things, and Mommy won't let him live here anymore." "Mommy ran away with another man; she likes him better than she likes us." There is nothing to gain by such statements, and the children will suffer from them.

Though it may be difficult, it is best if the explanation of the separation comes from both parents together. They can explain what the new living arrangements will be and mutually assure the child that they both love him and will continue to care for him. It is important to make it clear to a child that he is not going to lose either parent, even though one will be living elsewhere. It is also important not to force the child to take sides; there is enough pain in the situation without this.

The question often arises of how soon to tell the children about an impending divorce. The experts agree that it is best to tell them as soon as the decision to separate has been made. It is foolish for parents to think that they can hide their emotional distress and upheaval, even from very young children. They may imagine all kinds of things and worry if they have done something wrong, and it is just as well to let them know about the forthcoming separation and begin to deal with it.

3. Keep lines of communication with children open, and allow them to express their feelings. Parents may feel that talking about the separation is counterproductive—that the less said, the better. But it is better for the emotional health of parents and children to talk openly before, during, and after the divorce proceedings. If children are allowed to talk openly about their feelings it will help them to cope with the situation much better than if they have to suppress their emotions. Also, parents will be able to get a more accurate reading of the child's thoughts and feelings and be more able to correct his misconceptions and help him to deal with his emotions. It is unwise to ask a child to deny his feelings or to discount them. Statements such as, "You're not really afraid, are you? There's nothing to be afraid of." or "You're not really angry at your own mother" may make a child believe that there is something wrong with him for having these quite normal feelings. Instead of denying the child's feelings, parents can provide some outlets for them through activity and dramatic play.

Sometimes to protect a child from anxiety a parent will cover up her own feelings. But the words that are intended to reassure him are contradicted by the body messages. The mixed messages that are conveyed to the child are confusing, and as he tries to guess what is happening he may see himself as the cause of the parent's distress. It is much better for parents to be open about their feelings. This does not mean "unloading" on the child by giving him all the details of what is happening. But an honest statement from the parent that "I'm upset right now," followed by assurance that the child is not the cause, will be helpful. Being honest about feelings tells a child that we respect his ability to understand and empathize with our feelings, and this will generate feelings of self-worth.

4. Maintain as friendly a relationship as possible with the ex-spouse. Sometimes a parent will seek revenge for real or

imagined wrongs by using the children as a weapon against the marriage partner. They may continually talk about the other parent's failings and do all they can to present him/her in the worst possible light. Or they may even tell the children that the other parent doesn't love them anymore. The potential effects of such communication upon a child's self-esteem are obvious. A wife whose marriage has been broken up by the husband's infidelity may be so bitter and resentful that she will do everything possible to keep the ex-husband from seeing the children. But if a mother really has the children's interests at heart, she will speak as well as she can of the father and try to maintain a good image. This is especially important for boys, since the father is usually the single most important model of identification for them. It is destructive to a boy's self-image to model himself after a parent figure who is seen as bad and worthless.

Though it is wise to maintain as good an image of the other parent as possible, it is also important to be truthful. In the majority of people there are ample good traits that can be noticed. But what is one to do if the ex-spouse is one of those rare individuals who appear to lack any redeeming qualities whatever? In such a case the other parent would be advised to use whatever stratagem is necessary to keep him and the child apart. There would be no point in encouraging visitation if the effects upon the child would be all bad.

What about the parent who makes no effort to visit or contact the child after the divorce? As I am working with a child from a divorced home I will ask how often he sees the noncustodial parent, and occasionally find that it is seldom or never. In cases where the parent is a long distance away, perhaps in another state, one would expect the contacts to be limited. But it is not too infrequent to find parents less than 50 miles away—perhaps even in the same city—who make no effort to see the child, or even call on the telephone! It is not too hard to imagine how damaging it is to a child's self-esteem to think that he is so unlovable that the parent totally ignores his existence. In a case such as this it is important for the custodial parent and others who work with the child to be honest. It would be foolish to make excuses for the neglectful parent and try to convince the child, against all available evidence, that the parent really does love him. The blame should be placed solidly where it belongs; the child should know that the neglect has nothing whatever to do with him. Depending on the child's age, he can have a partial or rather complete understanding that the parent is the one with the problem—that it is the parent's lack of ability to love or to show love that is at fault.

Except in the case of the type of parent mentioned above, it is good for the custodial parent to allow and even encourage visitations. Too often a parent will try to sabotage the visitation schedule—either to punish the ex-spouse or because she sees a child's welfare as being jeopardized by contact with him. Difficult as it may be, the parent should help to maintain parent-child relationships and provide regular opportunities for mutually enjoyable activities. It is good for the daughter to maintain good relations with the divorced father too, as her later relationships with men, and her marriage, can be affected by the way she has seen the father's role exemplified. Hateful tactics against the ex-husband or ex-wife are cruel and unwise, and sometimes there is a backlash effect against the bitter parent. If, in spite of disaffection and separation, parents can remain friendly and speak well of each other, there will be a real boost to the children's self-esteem.

A very natural tendency, but one that parents should guard against, is to pump the children for information about the other parent with questions like, "Is your mother going out on dates with anybody?" "Does your Dad have a new girlfriend?" "What does your mother say about me?" Children should not be encouraged to be "tattle-tales."

Another mistake parents sometimes make is to use the children to carry messages back and forth instead of communicating with each other directly. Parents should know better than to expect that children can be neutral and unemotional and not be affected by the information that they carry. When they are used as message carriers children learn too much and get involved in the parents' problems, and it is upsetting for them to see the parent get sad or angry because of the message that is delivered.

5. Seek outside help when needed. Sometimes outside agencies, such as the church and the school, can be helpful to children who are adjusting to divorce. A teacher, counselor, school social worker, or school psychologist can provide a sounding board for a child to talk about his fear or anger. In group counseling sessions a child can find that he is not alone—that his peers have the same problems and emotions that he has. This knowledge can provide needed comfort and support.

6. Guard against false hopes of reconciliation. It is natural for a child who loves both his parents to want to see them get back together. Sometimes any friendly interchanges between parents are misconstrued as a sign that reconciliation is likely. Sometimes the fantasy persists even after one or both parents has remarried. To ease the child's pain, and sometimes their own, a parent may unwisely leave open the possibility of a reunion. If there is still love for the ex-spouse and a longing for reconciliation, it becomes all the harder to make the child see the inevitability of the continued separation. But to hold out false hope to a child is unwise; it only extends the grief and delays the adjustment which the child needs to make.

7. Look on the bright side, and help children to do the same. At best divorce is not a happy occasion. It is fraught

with anger, fear, and emotional tension. But it is possible to see some good aspects to it. If nothing else, the escape from the endless quarreling that usually precedes a divorce can be a relief for both parents and children. Some couples find that they get along better after the divorce; they find themselves noticing the good things about each other rather than picking at the poor qualities. Likewise the child may find that his relations with parents are much happier and rewarding when he is with them one at a time rather than together. One elementary-school boy began to see himself as having an advantage over his friends because they only had two parents and he had four (both parents had remarried).

Divorce is somewhat easier on both parents and children than it used to be because as it has become more common it has also become more socially acceptable. When I was growing up I was almost unaware of such a thing as divorce. The first time I can remember being personally affected was when, at the age of 11 or 12, a friend's parents divorced. I can still recollect clearly the pangs of sorrow I felt for this playmate; it seemed almost incomprehensible that such a thing could happen. Now, of course, even young children understand divorce and most of them probably have one or more friends from divorced homes.

After the divorce is final it is common for parents to have second thoughts and to wonder if they have really been fair to the children. They need to ask themselves if their children would really have been better off if they had stayed together. If they analyze the situation objectively the answer will probably be no. So rather than sit and worry and feel guilty about what they may have done to their children, parents will do well to move ahead with their lives with confidence and help their children to do the same.

8. Provide as much stability in the environment as possible. Children find security in a consistent environment, so it is important for parents to provide as much stability as

possible during the time that divorce is taking place. Predictable routines and rituals at home are important. It is a good idea to have familiar toys, books, and other possessions available to the child. It may be hard for a parent to maintain an organized household when under stress, but it will be helpful to them as well as to the child if they are able to do so. A young child who is striving for feelings of security prefers familiar objects and situations, and he may enjoy hearing the same story read to him over and over. Though the parent may get tired of reading the same story again and again, being able to predict what is coming next gives a child a feeling of safety.

We have seen that divorce is almost always fraught with serious stresses and strains for both parents and children. The effects of parental divorce upon the self-esteem of children are almost always negative. But parents who help children to understand and work through the divorce-related problems which they face will minimize these effects and will help them to rebuild a sense of confidence and feelings of self-worth.

CHAPTER 17

Self-Esteem in the Child with a Handicap

> In nature there's no blemish but the mind.
> None can be called deformed but the unkind.
> —*Shakespeare*

Darwin is an exceptionally good-looking boy of 14. He comes from a home of above-average income. An intelligence test revealed an IQ score of 126, which places him in the "superior" range. He performs well in school, being well above average in all academic classes. Though somewhat of a "loner," Darwin has one or two good friends and is not really disliked by anyone.

Blaine is a Downs syndrome child, age 14. He has the typical physical features associated with this condition. An intelligence test revealed an IQ of 72, which places him in the "borderline mentally retarded" range. He is in a special education program at his school and is performing at about a third-grade level in academic work.

Which of these boys, Darwin or Blaine, has the higher self-esteem? Surprisingly, it is Blaine! A closer look at their attitudes, and their home and family situations, may help to explain why.

Darwin's father was formerly a high-school football coach, and now teaches physical education. The oldest son followed in his father's footsteps and plays on the varsity football team. But Darwin possesses neither the interest nor the physical skills required to succeed in athletics. In a home where athletic prowess is prized he can't escape the feeling of having "let the family down."

Blaine has the "happy-go-lucky" disposition often associated with Downs syndrome children. He sees everyone as his friend and will go up and talk to any new person that he sees. At school all academic work is done in the resource room, with assignments geared to his ability level. In the nonacademic areas of school, such as music, art, and physical education, he mixes freely with "normal" children, who accept him quite well. Blaine's father has taught him to mow lawns in the summer and shovel walks in the winter, and he does a good job at both. He takes special pride in trimming and edging the lawns, and has built up quite a clientele in his community.

The Effects of Handicapping Conditions upon Self-Esteem

Self-concept is vulnerable in handicapped children for two main reasons. First, the handicap itself may prevent or make very difficult the attainment of success experiences necessary for self-esteem; and second, poor reactions and comments from other people may have an adverse effect. Sometimes the reactions of other people to the handicap are actually more of a detriment than the handicap itself.

We need to be careful about labels such as "retarded," "hyperactive," and "learning disabled." Sometimes we think of a child who has been labeled as having a particular handicap as different in all respects from "normal" children, whereas he is really only different in that one way. Depending on the nature of the handicap, a child may be able to compete well in other areas; physical ability, mental ability, ability to relate to other children or to adults, work habits, or healthy emotional qualities may be unimpaired. By stressing the things that a child with a handicap can do well, rather than the things he cannot do, we can help him develop a good self-concept. No one can be good at everything, but everyone can be good at something.

Since handicapped children are especially vulnerable to poor self-concepts, parents and teachers need to pay particular attention to the enhancement of self-esteem in these children. This is done through warmth and caring, providing many opportunities to learn and explore, and by accepting both the child's strengths and limitations realistically.

Exceptional children are likely to come into contact with many people—doctors, psychologists, speech and hearing specialists, and others. They are also likely to find themselves in more stressful situations than the average child. A loving home can help them to meet these stresses. Consistent routines and consistent structure in their life will also help them to feel secure.

The Impact of a "Special Child" upon the Home and the Family

Parents may experience a special shock and disappointment when they first discover that a child has a handicap. They wrestle with the questions "Why me? Why my child?" The mother may feel that she has failed in some way or has done something wrong. The father may feel cheated. There is often some mourning over the loss of the perfect baby that was anticipated, and often some guilt or denial. There may be a withdrawal from, or aggressiveness toward, the child. Some parents need counseling if they are to provide a warm and stable environment for a child with a handicap.

The presence of a special child in the home can put a real strain on a marriage. It is not uncommon for couples who have had an apparently good marriage to separate after the advent of a child with a handicap because one of the partners simply cannot cope with the problems involved. On the other hand a special child can sometimes have the opposite effect of drawing a couple closer together as they mutually love and care for the child.

Parents of a child with a severe handicap need to be careful that the other children in the family do not feel neglected. It may seem to them that all of the parents' time, attention, and even love are directed to the child that needs special help. One mother realized this was happening when her young daughter exclaimed that she wished *she* was retarded! It is good to teach children at a very early age to perform some of the needed service for the special child so that parents will have time to give attention to other family members. It has been said that we love whom we serve. By helping to take care of the needs of the less fortunate child, "normal" children can further their own feelings of competence, love and self-esteem.

The special child needs an emotionally supportive and stable environment. He also needs a stable set of relationships—persons he can trust and count on. He needs to get the message that parents are not unduly concerned about his handicap or the potential effect it will have on his future. He needs to know they love him just the way he is.

"Handicapped" Does Not Mean "Helpless"

It has been common traditionally to lump all people with handicaps together and call them "the handicapped." Now in the field of special education the advice is to not say "the handicapped," or even "the handicapped person," but "the person with a handicap." It might be even better to avoid the term "handicap" as much as possible and say, "the person who is blind," "the person who is retarded," etc. Though this may seem to be just a play on words, it does stress the idea that the person is foremost, and the handicap only secondary.

Children with handicaps can often accomplish much more than we might expect. An elementary-school principal once told me, "I hate it when a child has been classified 'intellectually handicapped' and has not yet been placed in a special program. A teacher may have been doing a reasonably good job with a child, considering his potential, yet throw her hands in the air when she finds the child has been classified as 'mentally retarded' and say, 'I don't know what to do with him; I'm not trained to teach mentally retarded children.'" A first step in dealing effectively with children with special needs is to realize that they are not all that different from "normal" children. This is especially true in the school setting, since we tend to be dealing with the mildly handicapped; the profoundly handicapped are usually identified during the preschool period and are probably in settings other than the public school.

A child with a mild intellectual handicap is simply one who scores below a specifically designated score on an intelligence test. He has the same basic desires and needs as any other child. He can learn and develop academic skills, but at a slower pace and lower level than others.

Sometimes we underestimate what children with various kinds of handicaps can accomplish. Don was born with an undeveloped right arm which is almost useless. But he does not let it keep him from doing anything that his friends do. He plays baseball, basketball, and soccer, and plays them all quite well. Don is a popular boy and holds a student body office in his high school. Once you get to know Don you forget about his arm.

Tim is blind, but he attends a regular public school. He has developed excellent listening comprehension, and he uses a tape recorder extensively. He is above grade level in all academic subjects. If you were to mention the word "handicap" to Tim he might say, "What handicap do you mean?" He thinks of his blindness as a minor inconvenience, not a major calamity in his life.

Level of Aspiration and Self-Esteem

The examples of Darwin and Blaine, mentioned early in the chapter, illustrate the fact that to a great extent self-esteem is a product of how well one reaches the goals he sets for himself. An early psychologist, William James, realized very well this relationship of self-expectation to self-esteem: "I, who have staked my all on being a psychologist, am mortified if others know more about psychology than I. But I am contented to wallow in the grossest ignorance of Greek. My deficiencies there give me no sense of personal humiliation at all. Had I 'pretentions' to be a linguist, it would be just the reverse . . . Yonder puny fellow, whom everyone can best, suffers no chagrin about it . . . With no attempt there can be no failure; with no failure no humiliation. So our self-feeling in this world depends entirely on what we back ourselves to be and to do."

It seems clear that one important way for children with handicaps to develop self-esteem is to help them to set goals that are appropriate and realistic. Goals that are either too low or unrealistically high can be counterproductive. Handicapped children, like all children, need to develop realistic goals out of their experience. This will mean accepting the fact that there will be some things that they simply will not be able to do. For example, no matter how strongly a blind or partially sighted person desires to learn to operate an automobile, he needs to accept the fact that this will not be possible. So parents and teachers need to help them to find things that they *can* do. It is just as important to expect a handicapped child to perform to the limits of his abilities as it is to expect it of a "normal" child. It also means that we need to cultivate in the handicapped child both a sense of social responsibility and a sense of self-sufficiency or self-direction.

Guard against Pity and Too Much Help

I first met James when he came, with his mother, into my office at the university where I teach. He intended to pursue a master's degree. As I talked to him and asked questions the mother supplied all the answers. During the year that he was in residence I seldom saw him without his mother. When he met with members of his graduate committee his mother was there to speak for him—and speak for him she did! She would call on the telephone quite frequently to get information and would say, "James wanted me to call and ask . . ." It was as though this graduate student were unable to speak for himself. When James was quite young he contracted polio, and it left him with a limp which the mother referred to as his "handicap." But James's real handicap was the mother herself, who hovered over him and did almost everything for him. The effect of this "help" and "service" to James was to render him quite helpless. He lacked confidence to do anything on his own, and his self-esteem was very low.

The tendency to coddle too much is increased when the child is more seriously handicapped. If a parent is not careful, sympathy for the child may turn to pity, and pity is damaging to a child's self-esteem even when it is justifiable and understandable. Rudolph Dreikurs entitles one of the chapters in *Children: The Challenge*, "Don't Feel Sorry." He says that if we pity a child, he thinks he has a right to pity himself. As he feels sorry for himself and relies more and more on the pity of others, and waits for others to console him, he loses more and more of his courage and willingness to accept the realities of life. The effects upon the child's self-esteem are obvious. Dreikurs says that a child who is blind, deaf, or crippled easily becomes the object of pity. It is almost beyond human nature to avoid feeling sorry for such children. But in so doing we only add to their handicap. Nurses and therapists who work with handicapped children marvel at the courage they often display and the cleverness with which they can overcome or sidestep a handicap, and are also very much aware of the danger of pity. They have seen children who had made progress crumble under the undue sympathy and loving pity showered on them by misguided parents and relatives.

It is natural that parents would feel sympathy for a child who has disabilities, but they need to guard against treating him with more sympathy than is really necessary. Well-defined limits are just as important to a handicapped child as to a "normal" child—perhaps even more important. They point out areas that are safe and those that are potentially dangerous. They help him to behave in ways that are acceptable in and out of the home. Sometimes parents of handicapped children are reluctant to criticize, correct or punish unacceptable behavior; somehow it may not seem fair to lay any more of a burden upon them than they already bear. While parents should show approval much more often than disapproval, to withhold correction of unacceptable behavior is harmful to a child's social growth.

The story of Helen Keller's early life is a graphic example of how parents may feel so sorry for a handicapped child that they withhold correction and disapproval. When Anne Sullivan was hired by Helen's parents she found a little girl who was totally undisciplined. She ate with her hands, threw things around the room, and did whatever she pleased. When Anne used forceful means to change this behavior, it was as hard on Helen's parents as it was on the child, and they almost discharged her. But she persisted and eventually succeeded in socializing the little girl. What a boost it was to Helen's feelings of competency and self-esteem when she was able to begin to learn and to behave in socially acceptable ways.

Accept Children's Handicaps and Limitations Realistically

At the other extreme of parents who coddle too much are those who nurture too little, not willing to accept that their children need any special treatment or care. A third-grade boy who was slightly mentally retarded was subject to epileptic seizures. Just prior to a seizure he would often perform some impulsive and seemingly uncontrollable action. For example, one day he was on his way to the pencil sharpener and suddenly jabbed his pencil into the head of a girl sitting nearby. The boy was referred to me, and after evaluating the situation I recommended special class placement in a program that was made-to-order for the boy. But the boy's father rejected any special program, saying that he wanted his son treated just like any other child and affirming that in his opinion he needed no special concern for help.

Some parents of handicapped children are not able to

accept the child's handicap; or they may accept it intellectually, but not emotionally. Secretly they wish for some
evidence that the child is really normal after all, or long for
a magic button that they can push to remediate the difficulty.
Carma, a child of borderline mental ability, had the misfor-
tune to be born into a very intellectual and achievement
oriented home. She had an older brother and an older sister
who were brilliant students. Carma's mother could never
quite accept the fact that she had produced a daughter with
below-average mental abilities. She would send her to the
store and say, "I want you to buy some bread and some
milk. The bread will cost 35 cents and the milk 50 cents,
and I'm giving you a dollar. How much change will you
bring back?" The problem was beyond the girl's comprehension, but the mother would become impatient or even
angry when Carma could not give her the correct answer.
How much better it would have been if the mother had
simply praised her for going to the store and not felt the
need to make an arithmetic exercise out of it. Experiences
such as this contributed to Carma's feelings of inadequacy
and low self-esteem, and she eventually developed deep
emotional problems that were more handicapping than her
mild intellectual retardation.

Focus Attention on What the Child *Can* Do

The child with a handicap is cut off from many experiences the parents would like him to have, and it may seem
that they and the child are in two different worlds. This
feeling is quite normal, but when parents accept the challenge they find that many experiences and activities can be
shared. The acceptance of this challenge is essential to a
healthy parent-child relationship. Then the emphasis can
change from what is not possible to what is possible. Games

can be adapted to the child with a handicap, and parents are often surprised to find how many games need no adaptation at all. There are many activities that the whole family can enjoy together, such as roller skating, bicycling, camping, and backpacking. Associating with other family members in these and in other activities can help to maintain self-esteem.

A handicapped child is frequently asked questions like, "What's the matter with your eyes?" or "How come you can't walk?" Handicapped children need to learn to deal with such questions. It will help if they know that most questions that are asked arise out of natural curiosity, not out of malice. Parents can help a child to anticipate such questions and know how best to answer them when they occur.

A child who is handicapped—emotionally, physically, or mentally—has the same basic needs as a "normal" child. If he receives love, and if parental expectations are realistic, feelings of self-esteem can develop.

CHAPTER 18

Conclusion

> If you wish success in life, make perseverance
> your bosom friend, experience your wise
> counsellor, caution your older brother, and hope
> your guardian genius.
>
> —*Addison*

One problem with a book like this is that instead of instilling courage and determination to be a better parent, for some it may arouse feelings of guilt or inferiority. There are so many things a parent needs to do to help a child to feel loved and capable, and to have a high degree of self-esteem. It may just simply seem impossible to do it all. Don't worry about that; it *is* impossible! The perfect parent does not exist. All of us make mistakes—sometimes fairly serious ones. But that's OK. Even the best parents handle some things badly and afterwards wish they could have another chance. And, fortunately, the second chance almost always comes, because that same situation will come up again in just a little different way. And when it does we can learn from past mistakes and handle it more efficiently.

There is no job in the world more important than that of being a good parent. Ironically, it is often the one for which we have the least training. Is it any wonder that most of us feel inadequate at times? Very few parents deliberately act in ways that are intended to be harmful to their children. Even abusive parents usually act out of feelings of helplessness and uncontrolled emotions, coupled with ignorance of what children are really like and what should be expected of them. Most parents can take consolation in the fact that they are doing the best they know how to do.

Seek Professional Help When Needed

In any home, problems can arise that are too serious for parents to handle alone. Fortunately, there are many resources available to parents. Do not be reluctant to seek help from trained professionals after your own resources are exhausted. Recognition by a parent of a need for professional services should not be seen as a sign of parental weakness, but parental strength. Counselors and psychologists in the schools are a good resource to you as well as to your child's teacher. Parents, teachers, and child specialists working together can remediate or at least improve most problems that children have. If the problem is more serious than the school can remediate, the school counselor or school psychologist can refer you to a community agency or private practitioner who has the expertise to help the child.

Increasingly, parents look outside the family for assistance in raising children. They put their children in special schools, send them to summer camps, and obtain special tutors. There is nothing wrong with providing special enrichment experiences provided the parents can afford them, the child will benefit from them, and they are not used as a substitute for care that the parents can provide. But if parents are placing on others the responsibility for caring for the children out of feelings of helplessness, they need the help that this book can provide.

Parents are often more capable than they themselves realize. Good common sense, intuition, and genuine feelings for the child will go a long way toward building bonds of affection between parents and children and producing mutual feelings of self-esteem. As parents feel more and more comfortable in their role of producing capable and loving children, the need for special enrichment programs and for professional help will be greatly reduced.

Go Easy on Yourself

Rome was not built in a day, and neither will you be able to make immediate drastic changes in the way you relate to your children. Nor would it be a good idea to change suddenly even if you could. Your children have learned to expect you to respond in certain ways, and they would probably become confused and perhaps even a bit insecure if they suddenly were not able to predict the results of their behaviors. Many times in our dealings with children we do not have time to sit down and calmly review all alternatives and possible consequences. Decisions must often be made right on the spot, and we are apt to respond impulsively and by habit. If you make a mistake don't throw your hands in the air and give up. Be willing to take two steps forward and one backward. Realize your human imperfections, and like and respect yourself in spite of them. Fortunately, effective parenting does not require perfection—or anything close to it. Children are resilient and can take normal foibles and inconsistencies in their stride.

Don't Give Up on an Idea or Technique Too Quickly

Sometimes a parent decides to try a new technique, and then, when the desired effects are not immediately apparent, gives up and reverts back to the old method, saying, "I just knew that idea wasn't practical and would never work." Behaviors that are learned well do not extinguish easily, so don't expect your children to always respond immediately in a positive way no matter how correct the technique you apply. Also, when you do change to a more desirable method of dealing with your children, apply it consistently. Otherwise the old method will still exert its effect, since a very small amount of reinforcement can cause responses to come back full strength. The gambling casinos in Las Vegas or Atlantic City provide a good example of how little reward is needed to keep people at an activity. The slot machines are set to dribble back just the right number of coins. If payoffs occur too infrequently, play drops off; if payoffs are too liberal, the house will not make the profits they would like to make. It does not take very many payoffs to keep some people playing hour after hour.

The human tendency to persist in a behavior with very little reinforcement works both for and against you as a parent. If the behavior is something that you want in a child, it is good to know that you don't have to give a reward every time in order for the action to be repeated. A child can be motivated very well with reinforcement occurring only 25 percent of the time—perhaps even less. The bad part is that poor behaviors can also be very persistent and difficult to extinguish.

When a specific behavior that has had a "payoff" for your child no longer works, he is likely to redouble his efforts, and things may get much worse before they get better. We can see this even in an infant. Suppose your baby has been conditioned to expect to be held almost constantly during waking hours, to the point that Mom gets very little done around the house when he is awake. Your pediatrician tells you that it won't hurt the infant to fuss and cry a little. So you decide that after all physical needs are met you will just let him play in his crib or playpen and not pick him up every time he cries. The first time you try this you manage to wait seven minutes, and then your anxiety builds to the point that you just have to pick the child up. Sheepishly, you decide that maybe you shouldn't have succumbed so easily, and resolve that you will try it a bit longer next time. So when the baby cries again you grit your teeth and manage to wait twelve minutes before picking him up. Still believing in your doctor's advice, next time you put in some ear plugs, but after seventeen and a half minutes your sympathy rises and your resolve melts away. The next time you busy yourself in a far-removed corner of the house with the dryer running, only to find the infant still crying when you return. At this point you may tell yourself, "This is just too hard! I can't bear to see little Charley getting so worked up and crying his little heart out!" And so you give in, perhaps just a little short of success.

Why was your attempt to let Charley cry it out not successful? Was the suggestion from your doctor ill-advised? Not necessarily. You actually reinforced little Charley's crying behavior by teaching him to persist in his crying a little longer each time. If he were capable of reasoning and could verbalize his thoughts he would be saying to himself, "If I just keep it up long enough Mom will come and give me the attention I deserve."

The technique of persisting in a behavior until the adult gives up and gives in can work equally well for older children. Mark has learned that no matter how many times Dad has said "no" to his request to go to the movies or to use the car, if he continues to persist, Dad will get tired of resisting and give in. Sally knows that if she sulks long enough Mom will let her get her ears pierced or escape from an assigned task. Do not be afraid to say ''no'' to your children and mean it.

The above examples are given just to illustrate that children's behavior can be persistent and not easily changed. Just as we learn to know each child and can often predict what he will do in a given situation, so the child learns to know us, and can sometimes manipulate us to his advantage. But what seems to him to be for his advantage may not really be so in the long run, and may mitigate against self-esteem rather than for it. Once you decide that a course of action is best for you and for the child, be persistent and give it time to work.

Put the Book to Use

This book can help you to evaluate your interactions with your children and learn to respond to them in positive ways that will enhance self-esteem. It will help you to anticipate the problems that may arise and be prepared to handle them when they do occur.

If, after you have read the book, you put it up on a shelf and never open it again, it will probably have little effect upon your parenting skills. Put it in a place where you will notice it and pick it up from time to time. The checklist which immediately follows this chapter is designed to help you to monitor the improvements you are making in helping your children to build self-esteem.

If you are a young parent you have a real advantage in applying the principles and methods outlined here. If you are an older parent whose children are almost raised you may be tempted to say, ''I wish I had tried some of these ideas when my children were young, but I guess it's too late to do much about it now." *It is not too late*. Self-esteem can be enhanced even in an adult. Start today! Learn to apply those principles that contribute to high self-esteem in you and in your children.

A Gift to You in Return

If you are already a parent you know that not everything about having and raising children is warm and delightful. Children demand constant care and attention; they get in the way; they often interfere with the parents' needs and goals. As one becomes aware of the sometimes overwhelming challenges and disappointments of parenthood, and of the time, effort, and financial resources that are poured into it, it is not surprising that some couples elect to remain childless. It is perhaps more surprising that most people do assume the parent role and find fulfillment in it.

Children help to fill the need that most of us feel for continuity—for life continuing on after we are gone. The act of creation—of bringing forth new life—is an awesome responsibility, but also a very rewarding and fulfilling process.

In the first part of this book I spoke of the invaluable gift of self-esteem that parents can give to their children. The effects are reciprocal. As good things happen to your children as a result of interventions you have made in their lives, good things happen to you as well. As you see your child growing in confidence and feelings of self-worth, your own self-esteem will grow and flourish.

A Checklist
for Parents

Many suggestions for enhancing children's self-esteem are discussed in this book. How well are you applying these techniques with your own children? The purpose of this checklist is to help you to identify those areas that may need improvement.

One way of using the checklist would be read through it and put a check mark by the items that you feel are in pretty good order—those in which you see little or no need to make changes. Leave the column blank if the item is one that you *do* want to work on. Then, over time, each time you look at the checklist again, put check marks by those in which you have made improvement.

You notice that there are two separate columns. Some parents may wish to rate themselves independently, each using a separate column. You may think of other ways to use the checklist. Use your own creativity, and make use of the checklist in any way that seems most helpful.

	1	2
1. I am striving to improve my own self-		

	1	2

esteem in order to set a good example for my children.

2. I model good self-esteem by pointing out my strengths and positive attributes.

3. I focus on the positive aspects of my spouse to my children.

4. My children know that I love my husband/ wife.

5. I tell my children frequently that I love them.

6. I often put my arms around them and hug them.

7. I kiss them when they leave or go to bed at night.

8. I do not attempt to control my children's behavior by withholding love.

9. I love my children for themselves, not for their accomplishments.

10. I make many more positive statements to them than negative ones.

11. I avoid making negative comparisons among my children.

12. I look for opportunities to praise them for things they do well.

	1	2

13. I provide opportunities for them to win at games.

14. I support them by attending all school and community activities in which they are involved.

15. I listen with respect to my children's opinions.

16. I allow and encourage participation of my children in family decisions.

17. I give special attention to them on their birthdays and on other significant occasions.

18. We have important family traditions in our home.

19. I express appreciation to my children freely and often.

20. My expectations for my children are realistic—neither too high nor too low.

21. I encourage attempts at self-reliance.

22. I refrain from doing things for my children that they can and should do for themselves.

23. I accept accidents and spills calmly and patiently.

24. I am patient and non-critical when my children perform.

1	2

25. I try to pay attention to the things they do well, and de-emphasize areas that are weak.

26. I allow and encourage exploration and encourage my children to try new things.

27. I allow a *normal* amount of messiness and disorder.

28. I see my children as competent and expect them to succeed.

29. I set a good example of assertiveness for them.

30. I teach them to say ''no'' to inappropriate requests.

31. I teach them to value their own opinions and to insist upon their own rights.

32. I challenge them to stand up to bullying.

33. I encourage them to stand up straight and look people in the eyes.

34. I teach them appropriate skills.

35. I help them to persist when a skill they are learning is difficult.

36. I teach my children to behave boldly.

37. I let them make appropriate decisions for themselves.

	1	2

38. I let them do things that involve *mild* risks and do not try to protect them from all pain and inconvenience.

39. I provide opportunities for my children to have money of their own.

40. I give them some freedom in spending their money so as to learn by experience.

41. I provide opportunities for simple decision-making at a very early age.

42. I do not allow my children to make their own decisions in situations that involve danger to themselves or others.

43. I make my standards and values clear to them and do not compromise them easily or capriciously.

44. I teach my children to avoid hypocrisy and to live and behave consistently with their own standards and values.

45. I model good decision making for my children.

46. I teach decision-making skills by exploring alternatives with them.

47. If one of my children rejects a value important to me, I do not let it interfere with my love for the child.

	1	2

48. I let my children choose their own friends.

49. I am polite to their friends, even those I don't especially like, and try to make them feel welcome.

50. I do not expect my children to fulfill my unfulfilled dreams.

51. I do not pressure them to make educational decisions or vocational choices to please me.

52. I show respect for my children's ideas and do not ridicule any of their comments or suggestions.

53. I gradually turn over more and more decisions to my children as they get older.

54. I spend individual time with each child almost every day.

55. I am developing some mutual interests with my children.

56. At home I interact very frequently with my children.

57. I really enjoy the time I spend with them.

58. I help with homework, but don't do it for my children.

	1	2

59. I remain calm and patient when helping with homework.

60. I spend quality time with my children at bedtime.

61. We spend time together as a family at least weekly.

62. I let my young children "help" me with household tasks.

63. I establish and enforce reasonable controls of my children.

64. I provide discipline, not leaving it all to my spouse.

65. I punish my children seldom and mildly.

66. I frequently apply natural or logical consequences in place of punishment.

67. I reward good behavior more than I punish bad behavior.

68. I am consistent (but not rigid) in my discipline.

69. I do not protect my children from the consequences of their behavior (except for serious and dangerous ones).

70. My spouse and I work as a team in discipline matters.

	1	2

71. If I think my spouse has handled a situation badly, I still support the decision and discuss it privately later.

72. I do not undermine my spouse's discipline (e.g., by excusing a child from a consequence or giving him something in secret).

73. I provide logical and consistent limits for my children.

74. I use a chart on the wall as a reminder to them of tasks that are assigned.

75. I use the same manners with my children as with guests and friends.

76. I treat my children with respect.

77. I avoid sarcasm and ridicule.

78. I refrain from nagging and scolding.

79. I teach my children to interact appropriately with adults.

80. I give them appropriate attention when other adults are around (neither ignoring them nor allowing them to dominate the scene).

81. I protect my children from embarrassment as much as I can.

82. I correct in *private*—not with friends or family present.

	1	2

83. I encourage my children to use the words "please" and "thank you," and model this behavior for them.

84. I am casual in dealing with my children's negative feelings, realizing that such feelings are normal.

85. I usually set a good example of emotional control for my children and do not take out my bad feelings on them.

86. When I resort to punishment it is for *behavior*—not feelings.

87. I allow my children to express negative feelings openly as long as they do it in appropriate ways.

88. I do not force them to apologize when they do not think they are in the wrong.

89. I help them find appropriate outlets for bad feelings (physical activity, talking it out, etc.)

90. When negative emotions appear I try to find the reasons.

91. I minimize fear and anger responses in my children by helping them to have more control over their environment.

92. I help them to overcome *mild* fears by facing up to them.

	1	2

93. I help overcome fears by re-conditioning (associating pleasant situations with the thing that is feared).

94. I let my children experience minor frustrations as a way to learn to cope with life situations.

95. I help them to cope with frustrations that are too complex or serious for them to face alone.

96. I maintain my composure when they are upset (for example, when a child shouts I refrain from shouting back).

97. I seldom raise my voice or shout at my children.

98. When I make a mistake I admit it and apologize to the child.

99. I deliberately ignore some attention-getting behavior.

100. I withdraw from temper tantrums rather than giving attention to them.

101. When a child is angry and aggressive I provide a "cooling off" period by removing him from the scene quietly.

102. I minimize jealousy among my children by giving each one the attention he needs.

| 1 | 2 |

103. I treat my children fairly, equally, and consistently.

104. I refrain from trying to talk them out of their bad feelings or embarrassing them because of their feelings.

105. When conversing with my children I listen more than I talk.

106. I use "active" or "reflective" listening with my children.

107. I listen to them "with both ears."

108. I let them know that their ideas are important and avoid negative comments about thoughts they express.

109. I minimize rebellion and resistance by using "I messages" instead of "you messages" whenever possible.

110. I make sure that much of my conversation with my children is positive and fun.

111. I encourage my children to look for positive traits in others, and to give genuine complements freely.

112. I encourage positive feelings for people of all racial, ethnic, and religious groups.

113. I help my children to select appropriate movies and TV programs.

	1	2

114. I provide appropriate help in the selection of books and stories for them to read.

115. I provide opportunities to associate with children of different religions and ethnic groups.

116. I discourage tattling and encourage my children to tell me about *positive* things they notice in other people.

117. I teach them to do things for others without expecting or accepting a reward.

118. Our family engages in projects to help the less fortunate.

119. I emphasize positive events and minimize the negative.

120. I teach my children the joy of service, and of giving rather than receiving.

121. I use praise and positive reinforcement to stimulate creativity in my children.

122. I teach them to believe in themselves and to be willing to risk and try out new ideas.

123. I emphasize the positive aspects of my children's creative endeavors, avoiding negative criticism.

124. We display our children's creative works of art prominently in the home (hang pictures on the walls, etc.)

	1	2

125. We have a large variety of creative materials in our home, and encourage our children to use them.

126. I frequently point out to my children the beauty of things around them.

127. I stimulate and encourage imagination in our children.

128. I guard against structuring their lives too much.

129. I enter into creative play with my children.

130. We set aside special times for fun and creative activities.

131. I encourage my children to write or tell creative stories.

132. I encourage good personal hygiene in our home.

133. I pay close attention to my children's diet.

134. I watch their dress and general appearance.

135. I guard against pity and too much help for my children.

136. I accept my children's handicaps and limitations realistically.

137. I am sympathetic when they are ill, without coddling.

Bibliography

Anderson, Eugene, et. al., *Self-Esteem for Tots to Teens*. Deephaven, MN.: Meadowbrook Publishers, 1984.

Battle, James, *Nine to Nineteen: Crucial Years for Self-Esteem in Children and Youth*. Seattle: Special Child Publications, 1987.

Berne, Pat and Lori Savary, *Building Self-Esteem in Children*. New York: Crossroad Publishing Co., 1985.

Brandon, Nathaniel, *The Psychology of Self-Esteem*. Los Angeles: Nash Publishing Corp., 1969.

Briggs, Dorothy C., *Your Child's Self-Esteem: The Key to Life*. Garden City, N.Y.: Doubleday and Co., 1975.

Clarke, Jean, *Self-Esteem: A Family Affair*. New York: Harper & Row, 1980.

Clemes, Harris and Reynold Bean, *Self-Esteem: The Key to Your Child's Well-Being*. New York: Zebra Books, 1982.

Coopersmith, Stanley, *The Antecedents of Self-Esteem*. San Francisco: W.H. Freeman and Co., 1967.

Dobson, James, *Hide or Seek: How to Build Self-Esteem in Your Child*. Old Tappan, N.J.: Guidepost Association, 1974.

Faust, Verne, *Self-Esteem in the Classroom*. San Diego: Thomas Paine Press, 1980.

Felker, Donald W., *Building Positive Self-Concepts*. Minneapolis, Minn.: Burgess Publishing Co., 1974.

Hart, Louise, *The Winning Family: Increasing Self-Esteem in Your Children and Yourself*. New York: Dodd, Mead and Co., 1987.

Kizziar, Janet and Judy Hagedorn, *Search for Acceptance: The Adolescent and Self-Esteem*. Chicago: Nelson-Hall, Inc., 1979.

Knight, Michael E., *Teaching Children to Love Themselves: A Handbook for Parents and Teachers*. Englewood Cliffs, NJ: Prentice-Hall, 1982.

Newman, Robert E., *God Bless the Grass: Studies in Helping Children Grow in Self-Esteem*. Saratoga, CA: R. and E. Publishers, 1981.

Price, Alvin and Jay Parry, *How to Boost Your Child's Self-Esteem*. New York: Western Publishing Co., 1984.

Samuels, Shirley C., *Enhancing Self-Concept in Early Childhood*. New York: Human Sciences Press, 1977.

Yawkey, Thomas D. (Editor), *The Self-Concept of the Young Child*. Provo, Utah: Brigham Young University Press, 1980.